THE KITCHEN GARDENERS' GUIDE

•••••

EDITED BY

DONALD J. BERG

Ten Speed Press

1☙
TEN SPEED PRESS
P.O. Box 7123
Berkeley, CA 94707

Book and cover design by ANTIQUITY REPRINTS
Type set by John Moses/Modular Compart Graphics

Library of Congress Catalog Card Number: 87-50126
ISBN 0-89815-201-1

Printed in the United States of America
1 2 3 4 5 — 91 90 89 88 87

FOREWORD

If you're interested in growing healthy, chemical-free food, if you'd like to try some vegetables that you've never had before, if you'd like your vegetable garden to be a bit more dependable and if you'd like to enjoy it longer, you've found the right book!

Last century, just about everyone had a "kitchen garden" as their only source of fresh vegetables. Before our miracle fertilizers, pH tests, hybrid seeds and chemical pesticides, our ancestors depended on simple techniques that guaranteed a good first harvest and an even better one with each new season. They grew a much greater variety of vegetables than we do now and they developed methods to extend their home-grown bounty throughout the year.

Those gardeners left us the legacy of good advice that you'll find on the pages of this book. I collected the articles from time-worn farm journals, seed catalogs, garden magazines and household cyclopaedias. If you're planning a new "kitchen garden" or if you'd like to improve an old one, I'm sure that you'll find their words as valuable now as they were when they were written. —— Donald J. Berg.

CONTENTS

• • • • •

• • • • •

ABOUT THIS BOOK

All of the advice that you'll find in this book is taken directly from 19th Century farm journals, books and garden magazines. In reading it, you'll be taking a firsthand look at the past and so you'll find many words that are not used today or that have slightly different meanings. To use this book you should know that...

COMPOST is typically a mixture of well-rotted manure with soil, ashes and sand. It was generally used as we use potting soil.

DIBBLES or DIBBERS are any pointed instruments used to make holes in the ground for seeds or roots.

DRILLS are lines scoured into the surface of soil to receive seeds.

HEAVY SOIL is earth composed largely of clay.

HILLS are simply the location where seeds or seedlings are planted. Unless noted, they are not raised from the elevation of the surrounding ground.

LIGHT SOIL is earth composed largely of sand or gravel.

NUBBINS are small, imperfect or underdeveloped fruits or vegetables.

MANURE in general, just means "fertilizer." There weren't many options back then. Typically, a manure pile was a mixture of stable waste, straw, leaves, weeds, household garbage and almost anything else that would decompose — just like our idea of a compost heap. The product of the rotted heap would be used to make "compost" or would be worked into the soil to improve it. It was not used as food for individual plants.

SPINACH and SPINAGE are the same thing. So are Salsafy and Salsify, and Cantaloupe and Cantaloup. The spelling of many words varied, in time, through the 19th Century.

Hints on
Planning & Preparing
Your Garden

Start Small

The mode of laying out the ground is a matter of taste, and may be left to the gardener himself, the form being a thing of trifling importance in the production of useful vegetables; and it matters not whether the ground be laid out in beds of four or ten feet wide, provided it be well worked, and the garden kept neat and free from weeds. One should determine what kind of vegetables he designs to raise as well as the quantity of each kind. If the object be simply to supply one family with vegetables, it is better to appropriate only a small plot of ground. It is far better to have a small plot of ground of only a few square rods thoroughly pulverized, well manured, and properly dressed, than one twice as large, and all these things alluded to, only half done.

By Thomas Bridgeman, from his 1866 book, THE AMERICAN GARDENER'S ASSISTANT

Where Should You Locate Your Garden?

The home garden in a majority of cases is a fixed affair, and no choice is left as the selection of site. While the condition of soil, its fertility, convenient lay and proper slope, are questions of no mean import, they are almost always secondary to the point of nearness to the house. The garden may be filled with good things of the season, but if half a mile from the house, compelling the over-worked and hurried house-wife to tramp such a distance every time she wants a supply of vegetables fresh from the garden, the cheering presence of young onions, radishes, lettuce, tomatoes, egg plants, and other vegetables will be missed by the family at many a meal that might have been more palatable and more wholesome by the vegetable addition and by the change otherwise. What good are the choicest things in our possession if we cannot make ready use of them?

The condition of many a home garden seems sufficient excuse for hiding it from sight. The best location for the garden is in a prominent place where it will crowd itself upon constant observation from the house. If well kept, it is one of the greatest ornaments to the premises, and source of everlasting admiration; if neglected and left to grow up in weeds, it will be a shame to the owner, an ever present accuser——a sort of conscience——and loudly calling for attention. A good garden is a sort of summer resort, to which the owner can take his visitors, and show them about with excusable pride; an inducement for an after-dinner or after-supper walk, affording opportunities for a few touches of improvement, for pulling up some stray weeds, or for the destruction of injurious insects, when thus encountered, for watching with pleasurable interest the growth and development of the things that are "new and curious." Nearness to the house means nearness to your thoughts and affections; better care and closer attention; more enjoyable and diversified meals; increased pleasure, health and happiness for the whole family.

By T. Greiner, from his 1894 book, HOW TO MAKE THE GARDEN PAY

◆ ◆ ◆ ◆ ◆

The garden should be as nearly level as possible, or, if sloping, not so much as to be in danger of being washed by heavy rains. If sloping, the slope should lie to the south, or as nearly south as possible. A plantation of hedge or evergreens on the north side of the garden will be found a wonderful aid to the earliness of the garden and to the hardiness of the small fruit plants and roots which remain in the ground all winter; if a woods or high hill be directly on the north and northwest of your garden, it will answer nearly as well as the hedge of evergreens. The garden should be so situated as to have good surface drainage; without this or expensive underdraining, it will hardly be possible to raise early or fine vegetables at any profit. These I consider the most essential points in selecting the plot for the garden; of course, a good, rich soil is to be desired, but the gardener, can, by the liberal use of manure and thorough cultivation, remedy a deficiency of this kind in a couple of years, while he cannot make a favorable location for early vegetables on a north slope if he should try a lifetime. By a careful study of the varieties in cultivation, and by trials of their merits in your garden and on your table, experience will be gained which will enable you to grow as fine vegetables and fruits on heavy soil as on light, sandy loam, and vice versa.

From the 1888 book, HOW AND WHAT TO GROW IN A KITCHEN GARDEN OF ONE ACRE

If it be practicable, make a garden near to running water, and especially to water that may be turned into the garden, the advantage ought to be profited of; but, as to watering with a watering pot, it is seldom of much use, and it cannot be practiced upon a large scale. It is better to trust to judicious tillage and to the dews and rains. The moisture which these do not supply cannot be furnished, to any extent, by the watering pot. A man will raise more moisture with a hoe or spade, in a day, than he can pour on the earth out of a watering pot in a month.

From THE FARMER'S NEW GUIDE, 1893

◆ ◆ ◆ ◆ ◆

Those who have not a garden already formed, and cannot avail themselves of such a slope of ground or quality of soil as they desire, must take up with such as may be within their reach. If practicable, a kitchen-garden should have a warm and south-easterly exposure. But when the ground slopes to the north and west, as is frequently the case, it is important to have the garden located on the sunny side of a grove, forest, or out-buildings. Every person, previous to choosing a location for out-buildings and a dwelling-house, should select the most desirable situation for the kitchen-garden.

From the 1866 book, THE AMERICAN GARDENER'S ASSISTANT

From a kitchen garden all large trees ought to be kept at a distance of thirty or forty yards. For the shade of them is injurious, and their roots a great deal more injurious, to every plant growing within the influence of those roots. Grass, which matts the ground all over with its roots, and does not demand much food from any depth, does not suffer much from the roots of trees; but every other plant does. A kitchen garden should, therefore, have no large trees near it. In the spring and fall tall trees do great harm even by their shade, which robs the garden of the early and the parting rays of the sun. It is, therefore, on all accounts, desirable to keep all such trees at a distance.

From THE FARMER'S NEW GUIDE, 1893

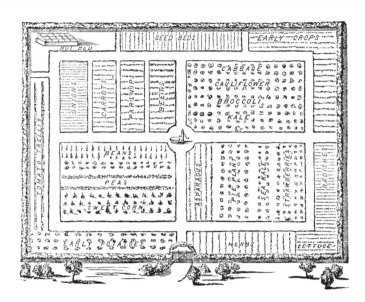

The Garden Plan

❖ ❖ ❖ ❖ ❖

Previous to preparing a kitchen-garden, the gardener should provide a blank-book, and prepare a map of his ground, on which he should first lay out a plan of his garden, allotting a place for all the different kinds of vegetables he intends to cultivate. As he proceeds in the business of planting his grounds, if he should keep an account of everything he does relative to his garden, he would soon obtain some knowledge of the art.

If gardeners would accustom themselves to record the dates and particulars of their transactions relative to tillage, planting, etc., they would always know when to expect their seed to come up, and how to regulate their crops for succession; and when it is considered that plants of the brassica, or Cabbage tribe, are apt to get infected at the roots, if too frequently planted in the same ground, and that a rotation of crops in general is beneficial, it will appear evident that a complete register of everything relative to culture is as essential to success in the kitchen-garden as in agriculture proper.

By Thomas Bridgeman, from his 1866 book, THE AMERICAN GARDENER'S ASSISTANT

♦ ♦ ♦ ♦ ♦

The most convenient mode of arranging the different kinds of vegetables is to; 1st, place the perennial plants in one bed, running the entire length of the ground; 2d, Plant the vegetables side by side which are to remain out all winter, so as not to interfere with next spring's plowing; 3d, Arrange side by side those varieties which require the whole season to mature; and, 4th, put beside each other the quickly maturing kinds, which may be succeeded by other varieties, in order that the ground to be occupied by a second crop may be all in one piece.

From the 1888 book, HOW AND WHAT TO GROW IN A KITCHEN GARDEN OF ONE ACRE

♦ ♦ ♦ ♦ ♦

If desirable, a border may be formed around the whole garden, from five to ten feet wide, according to the size of the piece of land. Next to this border, a walk may be made from three to six feet wide; and the middle of the garden may be divided into squares, on the sides of which a border may be laid out three or four feet wide, in which the various kinds of herbs may be raised, and also gooseberries, currants, raspberries, strawberries, etc. The centre beds may be planted with various kinds of vegetables, The outside borders will be useful for raising the earliest fruits and vegetables, and serve for raising and picking out such young plants, herbs, and cuttings, as require to be screened from the intense heat of the sun.

All standard trees should be excluded from a kitchen-garden, as their roots spread so widely, and imbibe so much moisture from the ground, that little is left for the nourishment of any plant within the range of their influence; and when in full leaf, they shade a large space, and obstruct the free circulation of the air, so essential to the well-being of all plants. Moreover, the droppings from some trees are particularly injurious to whatever vegetation they fall upon. When any plants require a shade it is infinitely better to make a temporary protection with wide boards placed on stones, or billets of wood, than to attempt to plant in the shade of trees. In the absence of wide boards for screening plants from the intense heat of the sun, two or more narrow boards may be placed side by side.

From the 1866 book, THE AMERICAN GARDENER'S ASSISTANT

If it were possible, I would prefer to have no fence around the garden, as it makes it much easier to keep clean. A fence is always a nuisance and waste of ground unless absolutely necessary.

From the 1888 book, HOW AND WHAT TO GROW IN A KITCHEN GARDEN OF ONE ACRE

◆ ◆ ◆ ◆ ◆

Where there is no lack of land, it may be well to make the garden of double size, so that each one-half (divided lengthwise) may be renewed and rendered clean from time to time by seeding to clover and mowing once or twice before it is cropped again with vegetables. Or one-half may be planted to potatoes, corn, or tomatoes, or other field crops, and the two halves used alternately for garden purposes. The great advantage of a thorough system of rotation can hardly be pointed out too often.

From the 1894 book, HOW TO MAKE THE GARDEN PAY

It is of great importance to rapid work and good gardening that all this should be arranged and settled in the gardener's mind, or better, plotted out on paper, before the first plowing is done in the spring. The plan being kept would be valuable in laying out the garden the succeeding year, as it would show just where each vegetable had been grown and where the different kinds of manure had been applied. If, in addition, the success of the various crops and notes of their growth were marked upon it, it would form a most valuable text-book for the study of improved gardening, each garden being an experimental station and each gardener a student in pursuit of knowledge and advancement in his work, feeding at the same time both physical and intellectual needs.

From the 1888 book, HOW AND WHAT TO GROW IN A KITCHEN GARDEN OF ONE ACRE

Garden Soil

Ground that has been worked in some cultivated farm crop, such as corn or potatoes, is more desirable for starting a garden than fresh sod land, as it is more easily brought into fine condition in the early spring; while grass is one of the hardest weeds to exterminate, especially among small hoed crops, such as strawberries, onions, beets, etc. Sod land is also often full of grubs, which work havoc among the strawberry plants and young melon and squash vines. In either new ground or in the old established garden, it will be of great advantage to put coarse manure on the ground in the fall, and plow it well under as soon as the ground can be cleared of the summer crops. The soil should be left just as it is plowed, without harrowing, leaving the lumps and ridges to the action of the frost. This will be found of especial benefit to heavy soils that are late in drying in the spring; it also adds a great deal to the appearance and cleanliness of the garden, as the weeds, old stalks, etc., are all cut off and burnt before plowing, instead of being left to scatter their seeds with every winter wind.

From the 1888 book, HOW AND WHAT TO GROW IN A KITCHEN GARDEN OF ONE ACRE

Drainage

As drainage will be in many instances indispensable to success, I will briefly state a few of the simplest methods that may be adopted, promising that it is utterly useless to expect to cultivate any soil satisfactorily that does not freely and rapidly carry off the surface water. An expert in soils can determine almost to a certainty, by digging down two or three feet, whether or not a soil requires drainage; but the safest guide for the inexperienced is to judge by the growing crops in his neighborhood. If on a similar soil good crops of corn, potatoes, or hay are found on undrained land, then it is certain there is no necessity to drain; for no matter how cultivated, or how heavily manured land is, there can never be a good crop raised in any season, if the soil is water-logged. If the place to be drained is of large extent, and the ground nearly level, it will always be safer to call in the services of an engineer to give the proper levels and indicate the necessary fall, which should never be less than half a foot in the hundred, and if more can be had, so much the better. In heavy, clayey soils, we make our lateral drains three feet deep and fifteen feet apart. Where there is less clay in the subsoil we make them from twenty to thirty feet apart and four feet deep.

RUBBLE DRAINS— If stones are plenty on the ground, they may be profitably used in filling up the excavated ditch to half its depth, as shown, and which is known as a rubble drain, using the larger stones at the bottom and smaller at top, and covering over with inverted sods, or six inches of shavings or hay, to keep the soil from being washed in among the stones, and thus choking up the drain.

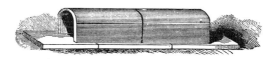

TILE DRAINS— when they can be obtained at a reasonable price, the best and most durable draining is that done by tiles. It makes but little difference whether the tile used is the round with collars, or the horse-shoe. We rather prefer the latter, particularly if the bottom of the drain is "spongy," when we use a board for the bottom of the drain, as shown. Here, again, great care must be used in covering up the tile with sods, shavings, or other covering, so as to prevent the soil being washed into the crevices and choking up the drain.

BOARD DRAINS— It is often a very troublesome matter to get the few drain tiles necessary to drain a small garden, and in such cases an excellent and cheap substitute can be had by using one of boards. Take ordinary rough boards, pine, hemlock, or spruce, cut them into widths of three or four inches, and nail them together so as to form a triangular pipe, as represented, taking care to "break the joints" in putting the lengths together. Care must also be taken that the boards are not nailed together too closely, else they might swell so as to prevent the water passing into the drain to be carried off. These drains are usually set with a flat side down, but they will keep clear better if put with a point down, though it is more trouble to lay them. Drains made in this way will last much longer than might be supposed. In excavations recently made we found wooden drains in perfect order that had been in the ground for twenty-five years.

From the 1887 book, GARDENING FOR PLEASURE, by Peter Henderson

Improving Your Soil

The soil must be well drained, either naturally or artificially. It must be rich; and the manure should be thoroughly worked into the soil. Plow the land in the autumn, and plow it again as early as possible in the spring. If there is any rubbish, remove it or dig holes and bury it below the reach of the plow. Then plow again, or work the land with a cultivator. This work should be done when the soil is dry and the weather warm. You cannot possibly stir the soil too much while the sun is shining. It lets in the sun's rays and warms and and mellows the soil. On light sandy soil, thoroughly and deeply plowed and manured the fall previous, there are many crops which can be sown to advantage without again plowing in the spring. It often happens in this latitude that five or six inches of the surface soil in the spring is thawed out and dry enough to work, while underneath the ground is frozen solid. If we wait till this frozen soil can be plowed, we frequently lose a good opportunity for putting in early crops of peas, potatoes, onions, cabbage, lettuce, radish, spinach, etc. And besides, the soil that we turn up with the plow, and which comes to the surface, and in which we sow the seed, is cold and damp, while the surface soil which we turn under is warn and dry.

From THE NATIONAL FARMER'S AND HOUSE-KEEPER'S CYCLOPAEDIA, 1888

♦ ♦ ♦ ♦ ♦

A quarter of an acre can be made equal to half an acre. You can about double the garden, without adding to it an inch of surface, by increasing the depth of good soil. For instance, ground has been cultivated to the depth of six or seven inches — try the experiment of stirring the soil and enriching it one foot downward, or eighteen inches, or even two feet, and see what vast difference will result. With every inch you go down, making all friable and fertile, you add just so much more to root pasturage. When you wish to raise a great deal, increase your leverage. Roots are your levers; and when they rest against a deep fertile soil they lift into the air and sunshine products that may well delight the eyes and palate of the most fastidious. We suggest that this thorough deepening, pulverization, and enriching of the soil be done at the start, when the plough can be used without any obstructions. If there are stones, rocks, roots, anything which prevents the treatment which a garden plot should receive, there is a decided advantage in clearing them all out at the beginning.

By E. P. Roe, from his 1886 book, THE HOME ACRE

♦ ♦ ♦ ♦ ♦

Many gardens can never be brought into a state of great productiveness on account of an excess of water in the soil. If the soil be heavy, and continues wet and heavy in the spring, let it be drained at once. After this, plough deep, pulverize thoroughly, manure highly, keep the weeds subdued, and in a few years you will have a garden that will produce anything that will grow in your locality. If the soil is heavy, haul on muck, sawdust, manure, in great abundance; and when such substances decay, the soil will be light, mellow, and productive.

The nearer the ground approaches to a sandy soil, the less retentive will it be of moisture; the more to a clayey, the longer will it retain moisture; and the finer the particles of which the clay is composed, the more retentive will it be of water, and, consequently, the longer in drying, and the harder when dry. But earth of a consistence that will hold water the longest, without becoming hard when dry, is, of all others, the best adapted for raising the generality of plants in the greatest perfection. This last described soil is called loam, and is a medium earth, between the extremes of clay and sand.

A light, sandy soil will be benefited if worked when moist, as such treatment will have a tendency to make it more compact; on the contrary, if a clayey soil be worked when too wet, it kneads like dough, and never fails to find when drought follows; and this not only prevents the seed from rising, but injures the plants materially in their subsequent growth, by its becoming impervious to moderate rains, dews, air, and the influence of the sun, all of which are necessary to the promotion of vegetation.

From the 1866 book, THE AMERICAN GARDENER'S ASSISTANT

◆ ◆ ◆ ◆ ◆

As some cultivators, by their method of using manure, show that they have very erroneous ideas as to its real object or utility, I would remind them that manure should be employed with a view to renovate and strengthen the natural soil, and not as a receptacle for seed. In order that manure may have a salutary effect, it should be thoroughly incorporated with the earth by the operation of digging or ploughing. When it is used in hills or on a given spot, it should be well pulverized and mixed with the earth so as to form a compost.

In the event of a scanty supply of manure, those kinds of vegetables which are raised in hills or drills, may be manured immediately under the seed or plants by applying a light dressing before the seed is dropped, being careful to cover it with soil, so that the seed may not come in immediate contact with stimulating fertilizers.

Much depends on the manures used on particular kinds of soil. The great art of improving sandy and clayey soils consists in giving the former such dressings of clay, cow-dung, and other kinds of manure, as will have a tendency to bind and make them more compact, and consequently more retentive of moisture; and to the latter, coats of horse-dung, ashes, sand, and such other composts as may tend to separate the particles and open the pores of the clay, so as to cause it to approach as nearly as possible to a loam.

From the 1866 book, THE AMERICAN GARDENER'S ASSISTANT

Ashes may be pronounced the best of the manures. They are also among the most economical; as, from our free use of fuel, they are largely produced by almost every household. Good husbandry dictates that not a pound of ashes should be wasted, but all should be saved and applied to the land; and, where they can be procured at a reasonable price, they should be purchased for manure. Leached ashes, though less valuable, contain all the elements of the unleached, having been deprived only of a part of their potash and soda. They may be drilled into the soil with roots and grain, sown broadcast on meadows or pastures, or mixed with the muck heap. They improve all soils.

From the 1893 book, THE FARMER'S NEW GUIDE

In plowing, a good, wide headland should be left at each end of the garden; it should be wide enough to allow the horse and cultivator to come clear out from between the rows and to turn into the next row, without damaging the plants at the ends of the rows by trampling and dragging the cultivator over them.

From the 1888 book, HOW AND WHAT TO GROW IN A KITCHEN GARDEN OF ONE ACRE

When Should You Work Your Soil?

◆ ◆ ◆

The following simple test will be of use to the novice in determining not only when to plow, but also when to cultivate and hoe the ground. Take a portion of the soil in the hand and try to press it into a ball; if it makes a ball and sticks to the hand it is too wet, while if it crushes hard it is too dry. In both cases, if worked in this condition, it will be left in a hard and lumpy state, that will take a long time to bring into good order. To be in good working condition the soil should crumble easily and finely in the hand, and should leave no dirt adhering to the fingers. It will not only give the best results when worked in this state, but it can also be done in half the time. Sometimes we cannot wait until the ground is in the very best order, as in a drought in summer, when it is needed for the second crop. In such a case it must be brought into as fine condition as possible by repeated harrowing and rolling; the latter is an operation too frequently neglected in the ordinary garden; every farmer knows the value of having the soil firmly compacted round the fresh-sown grain, and it is of equal value in every variety of seed sown in the garden.

From the 1888 book, HOW AND WHAT TO GROW IN A KITCHEN GARDEN OF ONE ACRE

Manure & Compost

A good supply of manure should be either made or bought, as the garden should have a good dressing at least two years out of three; the third year I usually use a phosphate, but would use the manure if I could spare it, using also a good dressing of lime every two or three years. The manner of applying the lime and phosphate is the same, but they must not be used the same season, as the lime will destroy the effect of the phosphate. They are sown on in the spring, after the ground has been plowed, and before harrowing, the harrow thoroughly mixing them with the soil. The supply of manure may be largely increased by pulling up the early peas, corn, cabbage stalks, etc., as fast as the crops are gathered, and adding them to the manure heap; this should be so located that all slops and waste from the house can be thrown upon it, so as to assist in keeping it constantly rotting; where corn stalks, tall weeds, etc., are put on the manure heap they should be cut into short lengths, with a corn cutter or other implement, to facilitate rotting and handling when the manure is drawn out.

If compost can be stacked in the fall and allowed to rot through the winter, it will be all the better. It can be composed of barnyard scrapings, well-rotted manure, chicken manure, or other strong fertilizer, mixed with at least an equal bulk of soil or ashes. This should be wet enough to rot thoroughly, but should not be allowed to lie exposed to the weather where its strength will leach away. When thoroughly mixed, I place it in old barrels under a shed and pour water on top of each barrel occasionally, to keep it rotting.

From HOW AND WHAT TO GROW IN A KITCHEN GARDEN OF ONE ACRE, 1888

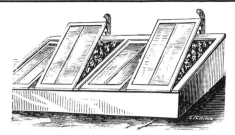

How to Build Cold Frames

Cold frames are simple affairs—box-like structures covered with sashes. The latter are the chief part, and involve the real expense in the construction of such frames, but being a staple article of commerce, and manufactured with special machinery in special factories, can now be bought at (or ordered through) any supply store at moderate prices.

The usual size is 6 feet in length by 3 feet in width, and the frames are made to correspond, namely 6 feet wide and 3 feet in length for every sash to be accommodated.

The selection of site is important. The proper place for frames is in convenient proximity to the water supply, and also in a position sheltered from the north and west, facing south or south-east. A close and tall hedge of evergreens affords a most excellent protection, but if such does not happen to be where it can be utilized for the purpose, a tight board fence, at least six feet high, must be built at the north side of the beds and extending their whole length. A building, hedge or board fence at the west is also desirable. In this comfortable situation construct your system of frames, making it as easly accessible as convenient for operation, and as snug generally as circumstances will permit. The frame is set on top of the ground, no excavation being required. The back is made of boards 12 inches wide, nailed to stakes driven in the ground at the ends and middle of each board; the front consists of boards only 8 inches wide, and fastened to stakes in the same manner, at a uniform distance of 6 feet from the first. When the necessary end pieces are adjusted we have a close fitting box, 4 inches lower in front than at the back.

From the book, HOW TO MAKE THE GARDEN PAY, 1894

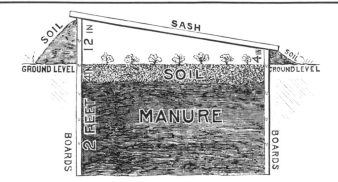

Illustration showing the manner of making the hotbed when sunk below the surface of the ground.

How to Build a Hot Bed

In making the hotbed, dig a trench a few inches short of six feet in width, or as wide as the sashes will cover, about two feet in depth and as long as the combined width of the number or sashes which you wish to use. This is then to be boarded up with rough boards, but they should be neatly joined and plastering laths or building paper tacked over the cracks, so as not to waste the heat. The back or north side of this frame should be 6 or 8 inches higher than the front, so that the rain may run off the sashes. The sashes held at an angle in this manner will also receive more sunlight for the front part of the bed than if front and back were level. The whole frame of the bed should be banked round with the dirt thrown out, or better with fresh stable manure, which will help to keep it warm and will make a bank to drain away any surface water, which, being very cold in the spring, would, if allowed to penetrate the bed, tend to chill the heat of the fermenting manure, and consequently check the growth of the young and tender plants, even if it did not generate that great enemy of all young plants, fungus or mildew, causing them to rot or "damp off."

From the 1888 book, HOW AND WHAT TO GROW IN A KITCHEN GARDEN OF ONE ACRE

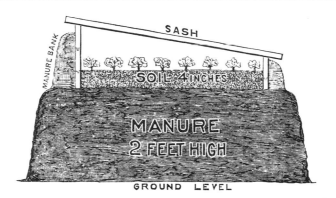

Illustration showing the manner of constructing a hotbed above the surface of the ground.

A Portable Hot Bed

❖ ❖ ❖

If there is plenty of fresh stable manure at hand, it can be corded in a pile two feet high and extending a foot wider than the sash frame on all sides; and when the frame has been put in position on the heap, the manure should be carried up on the outside nearly to the top of the boards, making a warm jacket for the plants within. A portable frame of boards is made for the sash to rest on, twelve inches high at the back and eight inches in front. This style of bed does away with any digging and secures good drainage for the bed. It would probably be the most satisfactory way for the gardener, who is also a farmer, as the bed can easily be removed as soon as it has served its purpose for the season, and the manure, which has become well rotted by this time will make an excellent compost for corn, melons, celery, etc. The frame and sash can also be set on a good piece of ground in the fall and filled with young lettuce plants in the early part of October, which will furnish salad throughout the winter.

From the 1888 book, HOW AND WHAT TO GROW IN A KITCHEN GARDEN OF ONE ACRE

A Simple Hot Bed

You may call it a hot-bed, forcing-frame, or anything else that you choose. The first thing to do is to dig a cellar about 10 x 12 inches across and six inches deep, and fill it with manure and earth well mixed. Now take a box without top or bottom, about 8 x 10 inches across and six inches high; place it over the cellar or foundation for the house, and bank the sides with damp earth; pack it down firm, and then carefully remove the box by lifting it out so as to leave the earth-walls standing, and make as many more as you choose in the same way.

"If you are careful, you will have the house all finished except the roof; but before you put that on you should plant some melon seeds, or any other seeds you choose. Now lay on a 10 x 12 glass for the roof—fix it on tight, so no air can get in. When the seeds make their appearance above ground, give them some air by removing a part of the south side of your house, or make a door and window in the back. Make your house in a warm part of the garden about the first of May. Let your plants have air as soon as you can see them. If you need to shade the plants, it can be done by sprinkling some earth upon the glass. In this way the plants will be kept from the attacks of 'bugs' while young, and being kept warm in cool nights will get such a start that they will be far ahead of those from seeds planted in the open ground."

From THE AMERICAN AGRICULTURIST, 1873

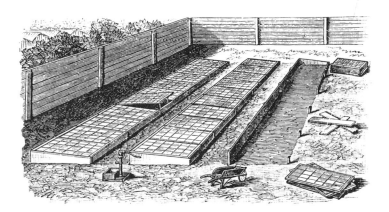

Hints on Hot Beds

It is best to locate the frames on the sunny side of a barnyard wall, or against a building that will shield them from the north wind and make a warm nook for them on sunshiny days. They should be situated conveniently near both to the manure pile and to a good supply of water, where they will constantly be under the eye in passing to and from work and will not suffer neglect from being forgotten or overlooked. It is quite important that there should be good drainage from these beds, as they are most needed at a rainy time of the year; dampness is not only injurious to the young plants, but it also takes up a great deal of the heat which should go toward forwarding the growth of the young plants. The sashes can be bought, ready painted and glazed, at the planing mills in most cities, and this is much the cheapest way to procure them, as they can often be bought for what the bare sash would cost in a small order at a country shop. They come 3¼ feet wide by 6 feet in length, and are 1½ to 2 inches in thickness, and if stored in the dry when not in use, and are treated to an occasional coat of paint, will last a lifetime.

From the 1888 book, HOW AND WHAT TO GROW IN A KITCHEN GARDEN OF ONE ACRE

Plan to Rotate Your Crops

Have you not frequently noticed that some people change their garden spots every few years? If you ask them why they do so, they will tell you that vegetables don't seem to do well there after a few years' cropping.

In starting a garden on an ordinary piece of ground, which has not before been used for this purpose, two or three years are required to get it pulverized and enriched sufficiently to produce a first-class crop, hence the necessity for retaining the same piece of ground for garden purposes. This can be done by adopting a proper system of rotation. It is a good plan to make a diagram of the plot used for a garden, and have it marked off into divisions of suitable proportions for the vegetables required. Each division should be numbered, or, what is just as good, the name of the vegetable raised there written upon it. These diagrams drawn each year should be carefully preserved, so that, by referring to them, one could ascertain just what had been raised on each particular division for years back, and by this means keep up a systematic rotation.

Such garden vegetables as rhubarb, asparagus, and others of a like kind, requiring two or more years to reach the proper bearing condition, should, of course, be given a permanent place for several seasons; but they, too, need removing about once in four years, in order to get the best possible results. They should never be so located as to interfere with the cultivation of other vegetables.

From THE NATIONAL FARMER'S AND HOUSE-KEEPER'S CYCLOPAEDIA, 1888

About Purchasing Seed

It is often a saving of several days to have the seed on hand, as it is sometimes impossible to foretell just when you will need the seed to plant a certain plot, how soon the ground will be fit to work, or how soon will come the opportunity, in the press of other work; if you have the seed at hand that part is always ready, and this is quite an item where the garden frequently has to be attended to in the intervals of work. Next, it is a cash saving to order all your seeds at one time. If, as is most frequently the case, you have to send to some large city for your supply, by procuring all that you need at one time, you have but one freight or express charge to pay. In making up your order, stick to the old varieties that you know suit your soil and your market; all the more if your market is your own table, for the greatest pleasure in gardening is in testing the merits of your fruits and vegetables with the appetites engendered by their culture. Also take into consideration the preferences of the household department as to the cooking merits of the different varieties. Do not experiment with your main crop of any vegetable, but do not neglect to try such new varieties as seem to possess merit, for the varieties are being continually improved by good culture and selection, as well as by hybridization or cross-breeding.

From the 1888 book, HOW AND WHAT TO GROW IN A KITCHEN GARDEN OF ONE ACRE

What Can You Expect from Your Land?

The editor of the Maine Cultivator published, sometime in 1849, his management of one acre of ground, from which we gather the following results——one-third of an acre in corn usually produced thirty bushels of sound corn for grinding, besides some refuse. This quantity is sufficient for family use, and for fattening one large or two small hogs. From the same ground he produced two or three hundred pumpkins, and his family supply of dry beans. From a bed of six rods square, he usually obtained 60 bushes of onions; these he sold and the amount purchased his flour. Thus from one-third of an acre and an onion bed, he obtained his breadstuffs. The rest of the ground was appropriated to all sorts of vegetables, for summer and winter use; potatoes, beets, parsnips, cabbage, green corn, peas, beans, cucumbers, melons, squashes, &c., with fifty or sixty bushels of beets and carrots for the winter food of a cow. Then he had also a flower garden, raspberries, currants, and gooseberries, in great variety, and a few choice apple, pear, plum, cherry, peach, and quince trees.

Some reader may call the above a "Yankee trick;" so it is, and our object in publishing it is to have it repeated all over Yankee land, and everywhere else. If a family can be supported from one acre in Maine, the same can be done in every State and county in the Union.

From THE FARMER'S EVERY-DAY BOOK

◆ ◆ ◆ ◆

Having the plan of work all settled, the next thing is to know what is to be grown, the varieties of each that are best adapted to the situation and soil of the garden, and where they can be procured of the best quality. Under this head come the seeds needed for the vegetables and the roots, tips and runners for the plantings of small fruits. This should be done as soon as convenient, as I have found by experience it is a great saving to have the entire supply of seeds on hand a week or two before it is possible to begin planting. This is an important item, as I have sometimes lost my crop from planting inferior seed purchased at the last moment from the commissioned seeds that are sold in the country stores. It does not pay to economize or try to garden with poor seeds; it is a waste of time and labor in planting, and a waste of ground and manure.

If "variety is the spice of life," it can certainly nowhere be more desirable than in the kitchen garden, which is to supply our table with its yearly demand for choice vegetables; I say choice, since every one having the care of a garden should strive to grow everything of the very best, and that, too, in great abundance and variety.

From the 1888 book, HOW AND WHAT TO GROW IN A KITCHEN GARDEN OF ONE ACRE

◆ ◆ ◆ ◆

The Vegetables

Have you ever tried Salsify or Jerusalem Artichoke? You might like them but you'll probably never know unless you grow them yourself. Although you won't find vegetables like Martynia and Skirret on your grocer's shelves, seeds are readily available so that you can start enjoying the amazing variety of vegetables that yesterday's kitchen gardeners grew.

The hints on the following pages are from 19th Century books, magazines and farm journals. You can tell the original source by the date listed: 1847 — THE FAMILY KITCHEN GARDENER by Robert Buist; 1852 — THE AMERICAN KITCHEN GARDENER by T. G. Fessenden; 1862 through 1881 — THE AMERICAN AGRICULTUR-IST; 1882 through 1886 — VICKS MONTHLY MAGA-ZINE; 1887 — GARDENING FOR PLEASURE by Peter Henderson; 1888 — HOW AND WHAT TO GROW IN A KITCHEN GARDEN OF ONE ACRE by E. D. Darlington and L. M. Moll; 1894 — HOW TO MAKE THE GARDEN PAY by T. Greiner.

The illustrations are from old seed catalogs and from the 1885 book, THE VEGETABLE GARDEN, by M. M. Villmorin-Andrieux. A reprinted edition of that book (see page 156) offers a great deal of additional information on historic varieties of vegetables and on planting instructions.

You'll find sources of seeds for any of the vegetables listed, starting on page 148

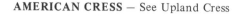

AMERICAN CRESS – See Upland Cress

ARTICHOKE – See Globe Artichoke and Jerusalem Artichoke

ARTICHOKE CHARD – *1881* – The leaves of the Globe Artichoke are someimes blanched, when they are called Chard, and used in the same manner as Cardoon.

ASPARAGUS – *Asparatus officinalis, 1888* – This is the earliest vegetable to be ready for use in the spring, excepting those that have been forwarded under glass. While it is quite hardy and withstands much ill treatment, nothing will better repay careful culture and generous feeding. One row across the kitchen garden would make a liberal supply for an average family. The seed should be sown where the row is to stand, and the young plants thinned out until they stand one foot apart in the row. This should be done as soon as they are three or four inches high and well started; if left longer it will be a very troublesome job. These young plants should have every encourage-ment of manure and cultivation, to make as strong a growth as possible; the stronger and faster they grow the better will be the size and quality of the shoots when old enough to cut. No shoots should be cut until the third spring after sowing and then should not be cut too long the first season. The fourth and succeeding seasons it may be cut from the time the first shoots appear until the first peas and lettuce are ready to take its place on the table. Then it should be well worked and allowed to attain its full growth, that strength may be stored in the crowns to furnish the shoots for the next season's cutting. As soon as the tops begin to yellow, and the berries to ripen in the fall, it should be mowed off close to the ground and the tops burnt, taking care that all the seeds are consumed; if left on the plants all winter the seed becomes scattered, and, owing to its capacity for sending up shoots, it is a very difficult weed to exterminate. I you do not wish the labor of sowing the seed and tending the young plants, a year can be gained by purchasing the plants. The one-year old plants are preferable unless the older ones have been transplanted each year, as they are gross feeders, and become stunted if allowed to crowd each other while young. To produce the large, fat shoots, it is necessary that the seed shall have been saved from the strongest shoots obtainable, and the plants fed

constantly. The best way is to cover the crowns, after the ground is frozen in the fall, with as much manure as can be spared, and work it down to the roots in the spring as soon as it can be forked in; or, if there are several rows, the manure could be placed on them thickly and the soil ridged over it for the winter by throwing up a couple of shallow furrows with the plow; this to be worked down with a sharp harrow in the spring. As soon as it is dry enough in the spring, the soil and manure of the bed should be lightly forked over with a manure fork and the surface raked fine; the reason for using the stable fork is that the tines are slightly curved, and if the handle is held in a nearly horizontal position the bed can be dug down to the roots, and the fork will slide right over the tops of the crowns without injuring them. Where more than one row is desired they should be planted about three feet apart, to admit of cultivation and free access to the beds for cutting. An advantage in sowing the seed is that the crowns are naturally established at a proper depth. In planting the crowns obtained from the nurseryman they should be set a depth of three or four inches at the most; not one foot under the surface, as is the common practice of truckers. Market gardeners cut the shoots as soon as the tips appear above the surface, so that their shoots are blanched for their whole length; but they do this at the expense of the table quality, as only the tips are edible in this way, and even these taste very much like old hay to any one who has been accustomed to the richness and delicate flavor of shoots cut at the surface when they are from three to four inches in height; this method has also the advantage of not destroying the young shoots just coming up, as the stalks are only cut an inch or so underground, and the knife only reaches the one intended to be cut. If the appearance of the blanched asparagus is desired, it can be much better obtained (that is, with less sacrifice of quality) by placing four or five inches of hay, straw or other litter over the crowns, which can be pushed away from the stalk when cutting and easily replaced. There is another strong reason for not following the deep planting, as usually practiced, and that is, in having your crowns so much nearer the surface they feel the warming and growing influence of the sun sooner in the season, and you are able to have your asparagus for cutting a full week earlier than your neighbor who plants deep.

BEAN — See Bush Bean, Lima Bean and Pole Bean

BEET GREENS — *1882* — There is nothing we like so well for spring and early summer greens as young Beets. If gathered when the roots are about as large as a Radish, and cooked, tops and all, they make a dish fit for a king, or any one else, are quite equal to Asparagus, and by many preferred to this popular vegetable.

BEETS — *Beta Vulgaris, 1894* — Rich warm soil (sandy loam) is the chief requisite. It is well-manured with rotted compost, and prepared as for other small vegetables, that is to say, plowed well, harrowed well, and made thoroughly smooth, if necessary with steel rake. In early spring when soil conditions and weather will permit, the seed is sown in drills from 12 to 18 inches apart, and clean and thorough cultivation given from the start. The crop is especially grateful for one or more applications of nitrate of soda, and can be largely increased or made earlier by this means. In the kitchen garden we usually have the rows 15 or 18 inches apart, since we prefer to use up the crop gradually, perhaps thinning at first for greens, then beginning to pull the roots when yet small, and continue using them as we desire for the table, thinning all the time, and perhaps leaving the last of the crop to attain quite a respectable size. For a succession, seed can be sown every two weeks until midsummer, if desired. A supply for winter use may be stored in boxes, barrels or heaps in the cellar, but should always be kept covered with sand, soil, sods, etc., to prevent evaporation, and consequent wilting, and shrivelling of the roots.

BLACK SALSIFY — See Scorzonera

BORECOLE — See Kale

BROCCOLI — *Brassica oleracea botrytis, 1847* — Broccoli is a variety of the Cabbage closely related to the Cauliflower, though not so delicate in flavor as that vegetable. It is supposed to have come originally from the island of Cypress, and was cultivated nearly two hundred years ago. In mild climates it is extensively used from November to March, the various early and late sorts coming to maturity in the very middle of Winter.

The seeds should be sown in April and May, in rich soil, on an open exposure, where the plants grow much stronger than near trees or fences. Sow the seeds tolerably thick on the surface; if dry, tramp them down and rake in lightly; if drought continues, give the beds a few waterings till the plants appear, which will be in two weeks. Transplant in June or July, when the weather is moist, in rows two feet apart and twenty inches in the row. If the weather is dry when planted, give them water every other day till they begin to grow. Their further culture is to keep them clear of weeds by hoeing and stiring the ground; when they have advanced in growth, draw some earth to their stems, which greatly promotes their luxuriance.

They commence heading in October and continue till destroyed by severe frost. The heads should be cut while they remain close, and before they assume a seedy-like appearance. In northern latitudes, it is necessary to put these plants into a shed or cellar, to have them during Winter. Lift them carefully before severe frost, and plant them in earth. They will head well when thus treated, but south of Virginia this vegetable may be had in perfection without the least trouble.

BRUSSELS SPROUTS — *Brassica oleracea bullata geminifera, 1847* — This variety of the Cabbage is supposed to have originated from the Savoy. It is a celebrated vegetable in Europe, especially near Bruxelles and other large towns in Flanders, where, from October to April, it is an every-day dish on the table of both the rich and the poor.

Sow the seed in April, and transplant in June, or July, in the same manner as Broccoli. The leaves of the plant are similar to the Savoy, crowning a stem about two feet high, from which grow out numerous little cabbages of from one to two inches in diameter. After the sprouts have been frosted (which is necessary to their perfection) they may be gathered. Immerse them in clear water for an hour, and cleanse them from dust and insects; then boil them quickly for about twenty minutes, using plenty of water. When soft, take them up and drain them well. They are then to be put into a stew-pan with cream, or with a little butter thickened with flour, and seasoned to taste, stirring them thoroughly. They may be served up to table with tomato sauce, which greatly heightens their flavor; or seasoned with pepper and salt, and eaten with any sort of meat. Plants for seed should have their tops cut off, and the little cabbages allowed to shoot, from which the seed is more perfect. It will keep fresh and sound in a dry place three years, but when grown for that object should not be near any other sort of Cabbage.

BUSH BEAN — *Phaseolus vulgaris, 1887* — An indispensable vegetable, of easy cultivation, growing freely in almost any soil, though in well-enriched land it will be more prolific in quantity and more tender in quality. It is a plant of tropical origin, and, like all such, should not be sown until the weather is settled and warm, and all danger from frost is past.

Sow at intervals of two or three weeks all through the season, if wanted for use. Seed may be sown in drills eighteen to twenty-four inches apart, and three inches deep, dropping the seeds at distances of two or three inches in the drills, and covering to the general level. For such as use them all through the season, three or four quarts would be required, although a quart at one sowing would give an ample quantity for any average family.

CABBAGE GREENS — See Colewort

CABBAGE — *Brassica oleracea, 1888* — Of this vegetable two distinct crops are raised in every garden; many gardeners, by successive sowings and the use of several varieties, have them fit for use constantly from early spring until fall, and throughout the entire winter by storage.

Early or Summer Cabbages — The seed for these should be sown in a hotbed from the 1st to the 15th of February. As soon as the plants are large enough to set out they should be given plenty of air, and should be gradually hardened off until they are able to stand the cool nights without protection; but they should not be allowed to freeze. Treated in this way they will be ready for planting out as soon as the ground can be worked. In making this sowing I would have it of two kinds——some of a small, hard-headed, early variety, and about twice as many of a larger-heading summer kind.

These early cabbages need very little care except to have frequent and thorough cultivation, as they are comparatively free from insect pests as long as they make a healthy growth. If attacked by the black fly or green worm, they should be dusted with plaster early in the morning, while the dew is still on them. The soil around these and all other crops that depend on quick growth for their superior qualities, must not only be cultivated, to kill the weeds, but must be kept loose and well stirred, to admit the air to the roots of the plants; it must not be allowed to lie heavy and packed after dashing rains, but should be stirred up as soon as dry enough. The rows may be as close as can be worked with the cultivator, say about three feet, and the plants about one and a half feet apart in the row, or even closer, if the variety grown makes but small heads.

Late or Winter Cabbage — As soon as the ground becomes warm in the spring, or early in May, a seed bed should be made and sown with the late varieties of cabbage and celery, or the seed may be sown in drills in the garden; the seed being sown in very thinly, so as to produce plants standing about half an inch apart in the row. Where it can be done, it is best to sow the seed in a special bed or cold frame, where they can be watered and nursed to a good size by the time they are wanted for planting.

It is important to get the seed sown early, that the plants may be had of good size by the middle of June, though they will make a partial crop if planted as late as the middle of August. As these varieties make larger heads than the summer cabbages, they cannot be planted so closely; the rows should be 3 to 3½ feet apart, and the plants 2 to 2½ feet apart in the rows. These can be planted and grown between the rows of early peas, corn or potatoes; but I would prefer to wait until the first crop of corn be cleared off the ground, as it can then be brought into much better condition. It adds greatly to the labor of harvesting the first crop when the ground is so closely planted, and the soil is apt to become hard and packed before it can be cultivated again.

When possible, the young cabbage plants should be set out directly before or after a good rain, but if there is no prospect of rain, they should be planted in the evening and a tincupful of water should be poured in each hole before the plant is set in; then draw the dry earth up around the stem and pack firmly around the plant; this will enable them to withstand at least a week of dry weather. If the drought should continue longer, or they do not come up fresh in the morning after a flagging day, they must be watered in the cool of the evening, when the plant will have the benefit of the water all night. It is waste of time to water them while the hot sun is shining, unless they can be shaded with papers, old pans, etc.

As soon as they become well established, the soil around them must be carefully loosened and cultivation begun. To obtain the best results they must be cultivated frequently and deeply. It is a common sight in some gardens to see the cabbage with stems two feet high and a small bunch of wormy leaves at the top; a closer examination will show that the soil is hard and trampled, and that the plants have been left to grow as best they may, while in the well-cultivated garden the stems are short and the heads are large and solid.

CANTALOUPE — See Musk Melon

CAPSICUM — See Pepper

CARDOON — *Cynara cardunculus, 1881* — The Cardoon is brother to the Globe Artichoke. Both are species of Cynara (the ancient Greek name), and are closely related to the Thistles. In appearance they are much like thistles with enormous flower heads. The Cardoon (C. Cardunculus), was introduced into Europe from North Africa, over two centuries ago, and though very popular on the continent, has been little cultivated in England or here. It is biennial, producing only a tuft of leaves the first year, and throwing up a stalk, and blooming the next. In good soil, the leaves will grow 8 feet or more high, with large, very thick, fleshy leaf-stalks. Some varieties are exceedingly prickly, while others are nearly spineless. The seeds are usually sown in the bottom of a well-manured trench, about a foot in depth; they are thinned to 18 inches, and when well grown the leaves are brought together and bound closely with a hay band to exclude the light and blanch the stalks, which requires about three weeks. The leaf stalks become very tender and crisp, and need careful handling, as they break readily. The appearance of the blanched Cardoon is shown in the engraving. The stalks are first boiled until tender, when the outer skin may be readily removed. They are then cut up and dressed in a variety of styles, with brown or white sauce and often with cheese. Those who become accustomed to Cardoon abroad are very fond of it. Those who eat the tubers of Jerusalem Artichoke, when cooked, will like Cardoon, the flavor being somewhat similar, though less marked.

CARROTS — *Daucus Carota, 1888* — These will be found very palatable as an ingredient of soups and stews. They are very easily grown, the seed being planted in drills and the plants thinned to six or eight inches apart. The seed should be sown in April or May, and they will be ready for use early in the summer. For winter use they should be stored in the manner of beets and turnips; they will retain their quality throughout the winter, and form a pleasant variety in the winter supply of vegetables. The rich yellow and red-fleshed varieties are the most popular, and retaining their bright colors when cooked, lend an attractive appearance to the dish of which they form a part.

CAULIFLOWER — *Brassica oleracea cauliflora, 1887*  — There is quite an ambition among amateur gardeners to raise early Cauliflower; but as the conditions necessary to success with this are not quite so easy to command as with most other vegetables, probably not one in three who try it succeed. In England, and most places on the Continent of Europe, it is the most valued of all vegetables, and is grown there nearly as easily as early Cabbages. But it must be remembered that the temperature there is on the average ten degrees lower at the time it matures (June) than with us; besides, their atmosphere is much more humid, two conditions essential to its best development. I will briefly state how early Cauliflowers can be most successfully grown here. First, the soil must be well broken and pulverized by spading or plowing to at least a foot in depth, mixing through it a layer of three or four inches of strong, well-rotted stable manure. The plants may be either those from seed sown last fall and wintered over in cold frames, or else started from seeds sown in January or February, in a hot-bed or greenhouse, and planted in small pots or boxes, so as to make plants strong enough to be set out as soon as the soil is fit to work, which in this latitude is usually the first week in April. We are often applied to for Cauliflower plants as late as the end of May, but the chances of their forming heads when planted late in May are slim indeed.

The surest way to secure the heading of Cauliflowers is to use what are called hand-glasses. These are usually made about two feet square, which gives room enough for three or four plants of Cauliflower, until they are so far forwarded that the glass can be taken off. When the hand-glass is used, the Cauliflowers may be planted out in any warm border early in March and covered by them. This covering protects them from frosts at night, and gives the necessary increase of temperature for growth during the cold weeks of March and April; so that by the first week in May, if the Cauliflower has been properly hardened off by ventilating (by tilting up the hand-glasses on one side), they may be taken off altogether, and then used to forward Tomatoes, Melons, or Cucumbers, at which date these may be started, if under the protection of hand-glasses. If the weather is dry, the Cauliflowers will be much benefited by being thoroughly soaked with water twice or thrice a week; not a mere sprinkling, which is of no use, but a complete drenching, so that the water will reach to the lowest roots. If the ground is slightly sprinkled around the roots with guano before watering, all the better.

CELERIAC (TURNIP-ROOTED CELERY) — *Apium Graveoleus, 1894* — Celeriac is merely a variety of the common celery with abnormal root development, and like others, requires good, rich, mellow soil. It is sown in seed-bed in early spring, and planted out in rows 18 inches apart and 6 inches apart in the rows. Keep free from weeds and well cultivated, neither handling nor earthing-up being required. The tuberous root is the part used, especially for flavoring soups, etc. Boiled, sliced, and served with oil and vinegar, etc., it forms the celebrated dish known as "Celery Salad."

CELERY — *Apium graveolens, 1847* — To procure early Celery, the seed should be sown on a gentle hot-bed, from the first to the middle of March. When they are three inches high, plant them out into a well-prepared bed of rich, light soil, which will be from the first to the middle of April——cover at night with mats or boards, to protect from cold or frost. By the first of June, they will be sufficiently strong to plant out in trenches for blanching. However, where extreme earliness is not an object, sow the seed about the first of April, on a rich, dry, warm border; when up, thin them out. About the middle of May, transplant them, three or four inches apart, into another piece of ground, to stock and harden, till they are finally planted into the rows for permanent culture.

The regular way is to select a level and rich piece of ground; dig the trenches a foot wide, ten inches deep, and three feet from each other; if convenient, from north to south, though any other aspect will do. Let the earth be regularly thrown out on each side of the trench, and sloped off. Five or six inches of well decomposed manure should then be worked full half-spade deep into the bottom of each trench. The plants which were transplanted into the beds or frame should be carefully lifted, and prepared for planting, which is done by cutting off the extremity of the roots; shortening their tops or leaves, but not so low as to injure the young centre leaves; and divesting the neck of the plant from suckers. This done, they may be planted into the trenches, at the distance of four or five inches apart; after which, give the whole a good soaking of water, and shade from the sun for a few days. Their after-culture, is to stir the soil frequently, with a small hoe, and giving a copious supply of water in continued dry weather. About the middle of August, or first of September, tie the leaves together, or hold them tight with one hand, while with the other the earth is carefully drawn up round the stems, but not so high as to allow the earth to get into the centre of the plant, which causes it to rot or rust. The soil for this purpose has to be broken, and well pulverized with the spade. If the weather be dry and hot, Celery should not be earthed up so early; in such case, a row for early use may be blanched, by placing a board on each side, and throwing the earth along the bottom edge of the board, to prevent the air from getting under. By this means it can be very well blanched, and ready for the table by the middle of September. I am aware that writers on the subject say, "earth it up every few days as it continues to grow;" but with such a practice in warm weather, it will not grow long, but rot off and decay. About the first of October, earthing up may proceed without injury; but let it be done firmly and evenly, and in a sloping direction, from the base to nearly the top of the leaves. In that state, it will remain sound for a long time. If continued frost be apprehended, dry litter should be spread over the plants, and a quantity lifted and laid in a bed of sand or earth in the vegetable cellar, in which it will keep fresh for several weeks.

CHERVIL — *Scandix Cerefolium, 1847* — Is a warm, mild, and aromatic plant, a native of Europe, and in olden times of great repute. After being boiled, it was eaten with oil and vinegar, and considered a panacea for courage, comfort to the heart, and strength to the body. It is much cultivated by the French and Dutch, who use the tender leaves in soups and salads as frequently as we use Parsley, and is considered by many to be a milder and more agreeable ingredient.

Chervil is an annual plant, and should be sown in March, April, and May, in drills, about a quarter of an inch deep, and nine inches apart. Cover lightly, and press the soil firm with the foot, rake evenly, and give a gentle watering in dry weather. The leaves are fit for use, when two to four inches high. Cut them off close; they will come up again, and may be gathered in succession throughout the season.

CHICORY (SUCCORY) — *Cichorium Intybus, 1883*
— Chicory is a very good salad, and one that can be had by everybody. Any one who has a small garden and can spare a little spot in it to sow a few rows, or make a small bed, has all that is necessary to raise Chicory. Sow the seed in the spring at the same time that Carrots or Parsnips are put in, cultivate clean, take up the roots in the fall, when other root crops are lifted, and store them in the cellar. Now the roots should be potted. Large flower-pots, nail kegs, flour barrels cut in two, boxes or tubs of most any kind will answer the purpose if they are deep enough to allow the roots to go down through the soil. A very large flower-pot would hold nearly a dozen good roots, a large box or tub would hold, perhaps, two dozen. The roots can be put in to grow at intervals of one to two weeks all through the winter, as the tops may be consumed. To have the leaves nicely blanched they should be grown in a place nearly dark; a warm cellar is a very good place, a warm closet, or any warm corner where 50° of heat can be had, will do. Give water when the roots are first placed in the soil, and afterward as may be needed, not allowing the soil to become dry. The leaves grow very rapidly borne on their long cream-colored stalks, which are unsurpassed as a good salad.

CHIVES — *Allium Schaenoprasum, 1864* — This humble member of the onion genus is one of those old fashioned things which but few think of planting, but which is always acceptable in its season to those who are fond of onions in any form. It is perfectly hardy, being found growing wild in the vicinity of the great Lakes and northward; it is also a native of Europe. The small onion-like bulbs throw up early in spring their tufts of small cylindrical leaves, and later in the season a small umbel of flowers. The plant multiplies very rapidly by the root, and like many other plants which do this, the chives, in the cultivated state at least, have only barren flowers. The engraving shows the plant of about two thirds the natural size, and it will be seen that it is very much like a miniature onion. The young and tender leaves are the part used, and they are much prized by many to flavor salads, soups, omelettes, and for any other purpose for which onions are used. They are sometimes eaten dressed with vinegar in the same manner as young onions. Its flavor is more delicate than that of any variety of the onion, and where needed merely as a seasoning may in most cases be substituted for it. Chives are propagated by setting small clusters of the bulbs at distances of six inches, in rows a foot apart. They are sometimes set as edging to paths in the kitchen garden, and are well adapted to this purpose. Whether the leaves are needed for use or not, the plant should be cut over frequently to keep the growth young and fresh. In a few years a single bulb will multiply to form a clump six or eight inches in diameter. At the fourth or fifth year after setting, the clumps should be taken up and the planting renewed.

COLEWORT (COLLARD, CABBAGE GREENS) — *Brassica oleracea, 1894* — Nothing more nor less than common cabbage used while young. It seems to me that one might be satisfied with the good American name "cabbage greens," and as such they are known and used quite commonly in the southern states. Cabbage seed is sown thickly in rows a foot apart, cultivated as if grown for plants, and cut and used when about 8 inches high.

CORN (INDIAN CORN, SWEET CORN) — *Zea Mays, 1894* — The first sweet corn should be planted early in April, and should be of some small-growing, very early variety. This corn will have to struggle with the frost and chilling nights but will be ready for use long before any of the really fine kinds can be had.

About the third week in April a second sowing of this early corn should be made, and at the same time should be planted some early large-eared variety and an equal amount of a later variety. Thereafter a planting should be made every ten days or two weeks, of a favorite sort, which, with me, is Stowell's Evergreen, although I plant other kinds throughout the season, for the sake of variety. These plantings should be kept up until the 10th of July, after which the late kinds will hardly mature; but if the ground can be spared, I would keep on planting until the 10th of August, as, if the fall should be late, the corn that has well-set ears that have not yet ripened should be cut off at the ground and stacked against the south side of a fence or building; it should be stood up nearly two feet in thickness, to prevent freezing, but should not be thicker, as it will heat too much and will be awkward to handle when sorting over for the good ears. Treated in this way it will provide ears for use well into November, but of course they will not be of as fine a quality as those matured in the ordinary way.

As the earliest varieties only grow about three feet high and have the ears set close to the ground, the best way of planting them is to drop the seed ten inches to one foot apart, in drills. Sow plenty of seed, and if it comes up too thickly it can easily be thinned out when hoeing; all suckers should be broken off at the same time, so as to throw the strength of the plants into the ears.

If two rows are planted across the garden at each planting they will furnish an ample supply for the average family, If it is needed for canning or drying, an extra large planting should be made early in May, which will mature after the heavy harvest work is over and before the fall fruit is ready to preserve.

If some fine compost is placed in the drills or hills, it will help greatly to give the young plants a good start until they can reach the manure with which the garden has been dressed; where this compost is put in it should be covered with an inch of soil before the seed is sown.

The climbing snap beans may be planted in the hill with the tall-growing corn, or hills of pumpkins; squashes or cucumbers may be made in every fourth hill and every third row, although the vines will be very much in the way of continued cultivation if the ground is inclined to be weedy. Sweet corn should not be planted within one hundred yards of field or pop-corn, as the pollen will be sure to mix and spoil the quality of the table corn. It will sometimes mix at greater distances, but this distance would be safe in most cases.

CORN SALAD (FETTICUS, LAMBS' LETTUCE, VETTICOST) — *Valerianella olitoria or Fedia olitoria, 1847* — Fetticus or Lambs' Lettuce is a native of Europe, and cultivated extensively as a Spring salad, but in France they frequently dress it like Spinach. It is called Lambs' Lettuce, from its having been in repute as an early feed for lambs. Every garden should have a patch of this very palatable vegetable, as it comes early in Spring, when even the sight of green is refreshing.

Sow the seed from the 8th to the 20th of September, in shallow drills, one-fourth inch deep and six inches apart; cover lightly, and if dry weather, tread or roll the ground to press the seed and soil together. It is an annual, and requires to be sown every year. Hoe and keep clear of weeds; in November cover slightly with straw; when wanted, the leaves should be picked and not cut. If the Winter proves mild, it will be in use the whole season. If the seed is not fresh every year, it will frequently lie six months in the ground before it vegetates. It requires good rich soil; on such the flavor is greatly improved.

CRESS (PEPPERGRASS) — *Lepidum Sativum, 1894* — No vegetable starts quicker from seed or is easier to grow if the flea beetle is kept off. The leaves have a very pungent taste, and are much used as a salad, usually as a condiment with lettuce and other salad materials. Sow seed thickly in drills one foot apart, guard against flea beetle depredations while the plants are small, and cut as desired. The plants run to seed quickly, and frequent successive sowings must be made, if a constant supply is wanted.

CUCUMBER — *Cucumis sativis, 1882* — In this country we can grow Cucumbers without much trouble and expense, especially the small, native varieties, though, if an early crop is desired, artificial heat must be used. One of the best methods is the ordinary hot-bed, and if this is managed properly, the result will be highly satisfactory. The Cucumber will bear almost any amount of heat, if accompanied with sufficient moisture. Cold nights are most to be dreaded by the gardener, and here many fail. Give no air chilly nights, and cover the glass in severe weather with mats, or something of the kind, otherwise you will soon notice the leaves turning yellow and looking sickly. After the vines have filled the frame, if the weather is mild, it can be raised by putting blocks or bricks at the corners, thus allowing the vines to escape and find room for growth. Later, the frame and glass may be entirely removed, but abundance of water must be given, for the Cucumber likes rich food and plenty of water.

For a second crop I merely place a barrowful of manure for each hill, raising the hill some six inches above the surface. After planting the seed I put a hand-glass over it. This may be a simple box, with a light or two of glass on top, which protects from wind, and is especially beneficial cold nights. When the plants commence to run, the boxes may be raised like the hot-bed frame. When glass is used, it is sometimes necessary to shade in bright suns, or the leaves will burn, and also give a little air, but be careful of draughts, for the vines will take cold as easily as a person perspiring in a warm room.

For the last crop, for pickling and the like, I merely put seed in hills in a good, rich, warm soil, about as I would Corn.

Pick fruit young, and never allow any to go to seed, or the crop will be injured. Pinch off the tops of the leading shoots if grown under glass, as it induces fruitfulness, but I never take this trouble with field crops.

DANDELION — *Leontodon Taraxacum, 1852* — This is a hardy perennial plant, which is found growing spontaneously in Great Britain and the United States. It might easily be propagated either by seeds or roots, and, if introduced as a garden plant, should have a rich, deep soil, and be carefully tied up and earthed round to blanch it effectually. Cut off all the flowers as they appear, to prevent the dispersion of the seed and the weakening of the plant. When salad is scarce, the dandelion might be dug up from road-sides in winter, and forced in pots like succory.

The leaves in early spring, when just unfolding, afford a very good ingredient in salads. The French sometimes eat the young roots, and the etiolated [blanched or whitened] leaves with thin slices of bread and butter. When blanched, the leaves considerably resemble those of endive in taste. The root is considered an equally good substitute for coffee as chicory, and may, like that plant, be stored in cellars and barrels, for producing winter salad.

EGG-PLANT (GUINEA SQUASH) — *Solanum Melongena, 1847* — The Egg-Plant was introduced from Africa, and is called by some the Guinea Squash. It is generally cultivated, and becoming more so every year. They are cut into thin slices and fried, and have a taste very similar to oysters. Others use them in stews and soups. They are fit for the kitchen when they attain the size of a goose egg, and are in use till they become nearly ripe, which is easily known by the seeds changing to a brown color. Many individuals are exceedingly fond of them, while others will not taste them in any form.

There is a great ambition among growers to have this vegetable in early use. I delight to encourage this emulation whenever it is manifested. Competition promotes industry, and industry promotes health. Man possessing these ingredients is very rarely unhappy. Sow the seeds on a gentle hot-bed about the first of March, on a rich, light soil; give a good watering, and keep the frame close for a few days till the seed comes up. Be careful to give the soil a sprinkling of water whenever it appears to be dry. As soon as the plants grow, give air freely, covering the glass in cold nights. When they attain the height of two inches, thin them out to three inches apart, or transplant them into another bed. Where there is plenty of room, the latter is the best method. They can be transplanted out from the 1st to the 15th of May, into a warm border of rich ground, from whence the early Lettuce or Radishes have been taken. Give a good watering after being removed; hoe well; keep clean; as they grow draw earth to their stems. They will cut about the end of June or 1st of July. For a late crop, sow in April, on a warm border where they are to remain, or transplant in June during moist weather. Plant in rows two feet apart, and two feet from plant to plant.

ENDIVES — *Cichorium Endivia, 1862* — Green salads  are, at all seasons of the year, very refreshing and healthful articles of food. At the very head stands lettuce, particularly those kinds which form heads readily; but few or no kinds will bear the heat of Summer. They will not head, acquire a disagreeable bitter taste, and are tough. The delicious salad named above comes in to supply the place of lettuce during the heats of August, and remains in perfection during the Autumn and Winter. It may be sowed at any time during the Summer, up to the first week in August, needing good deep rich garden soil, frequently stirred. There are several kinds. We prefer the broad-leafed variety. Sow in drills, and transplant 12 to 14 inches apart. As the plants grow they may be watered with liquid manure, and if the ground is well and frequently hoed, they will grow rapidly, spreading out a mass of leaves, lying flat on the ground, 12 to 14 inches in diameter.

If wanted for summer use, when they have attained the size of a dining-plate, the leaves are gathered together when dry, and tied with a piece of bass-matting or string. After a heavy rain, should one occur by which the inside of the plants are wet, they must be unbound and opened to dry in the middle of the day, and bound up again before the effect of the bleaching is lost. The blanched portions form a very pleasant summer and autumn salad. The chief excellence of the endive is seen in Winter.

After frosts have cut down tender things in the garden, we pull up the endives, remove any decayed leaves, and set them out in the sand-beds in the cellar, closely packed together. Very soon they begin to grow, and the new growth is beautifully blanched, while that tenderer portion of the older growth bleaches also. The largest and most vigorous plants are earliest fit for the table, and others follow in succession.

FENNEL — *Anethum Faeniculum, 1847* — This is a native of Europe, and may be seen growing wild on the banks of rivers and near the sea coasts. It is an indispensable ingredient in French cookery, and extensively used by the English, but comparatively in little demand with us. Its tender stalks are used in soups and fish sauces, also as garnishes for dishes.

Fennel is cultivated by sowing the seeds early in Spring, in shallow drills half an inch deep and ten inches wide, covering with fine earth. They should be sown where they are intended to grow. Thin out the plants for four inches apart; a dozen of good roots will supply any family, and when once established, there is little fear of losing it, being a perennial and will last many years. Seedlings will also come up plentifully around the old plants, though it is not advisable to allow the plants to go to seed unless it is wanted for use. If the flower stems are cut off as soon as they appear, it will encourage a production of young leaves below.

FETTICUS — See Corn Salad

GARLIC — *Allium Sativum, 1847* — Garlic is a native of many parts of the world, and has been in general use for two centuries. Many very excellent and medicinal qualities are attributed to its root, and it would no doubt be more generally used if it were not for its unpleasant odor. The French use it in sauces and salads.

There are two varieties cultivated, under the name of Large and Small. As either of them is large enough for any purpose, one variety only is necessary. The root is a bulb, divided into parts called psuedo-bulbs or cloves. It is propagated by planting these cloves in drills two inches deep, six inches apart, and four inches from plant to plant, early in Spring, on light, rich ground. It requires to be frequently hoed and kept free from weeds. About the end of July the bulbs are generally full grown, which will be evident from the yellow appearance and withering of the leaves. They must then be taken up, cleaned and dried, and afterwards tied in bundles. to be hung up in a shed or room and preserved for use.

GLOBE ARTICHOKE — *Cynara scolymus, 1886* — This is of easy culture, doing best when grown in a deep, loamy soil, one that has been thoroughly enriched with well decayed manure, and if possible, give a dressing of wood ashes with a sprinkling of salt, and harrow it in thoroughly.

As the Artichoke is a perennial plant, a bed, after being once established, will last for many years, if properly cared for and protected during the winter season, by covering with six inches of leaves or coarse, littery manure. The seed should be sown as early in the spring as possible, in drills about one foot apart, and the young plants should be well cultivated until they are strong enough to handle——say five or six inches in height, when they can be transplanted into permanent beds prepared as above advised. They should be placed in rows about three feet apart, the plants standing about two feet distant in the row. Planting is best done just after rain, care being taken to firm the soil well about the plants, but if the ground is dry they should be freely watered until growth commences. The plantation will only give a partial crop the first season, the second furnishing the largest and best, and where the Artichoke is in demand, I think that it is an excellent plan to make a planting every second season, and this can be done by carefully removing the suckers from the old roots in April or May, and treating them as advised for spring sown plants.

GROUND PEA — See Peanut

GUINEA SQUASH — See Egg-Plant

GUMBO — See Okra

HORSE RADISH — *Cochiearia armoracea, 1886* — The best is grown by planting 8-inch lengths of root grown the previous year. These young roots planted in spring, small end down, with the top two inches below the surface, in rich, well-cultivated soil, will form radish of large size and superior quality, in one season's growth. After having several weeks' growth rub off the young side roots from the newly-planted roots, to increase the size and insure a smooth, well-shaped root. See to it that no roots are scattered about the garden, as every piece of root, however small it may be, will, in a short time, become a strong plant, difficult to eradicate, and thus prove how annoying a good thing is in the wrong place.

INDIAN CORN — See Corn

INDIAN CRESS — See Nasturtium

JERUSALEM ARTICHOKE — *Helianthus tuberosus, 1847* — The tuberous-rooted Sunflower native of South America, and has been cultivated for two centuries. Like many other new vegetables, when first introduced, it was extolled extravagantly. It was baked in pies, with dates, ginger, raisins, &c.; and of

course amalgamated with such good things that it could not taste indifferently. When boiled in the simple way of Potatoes, however, they will not form a very palatable dish. The modern way of serving them up, is to boil them till they become tender, when, after being peeled and stewed with butter and wine, they are considered pleasant, and taste similar to the true Artichoke.

They are propagated and planted in the same manner as the Potatoe, any time in March and will grow in any soil, even under trees. They are best fresh planted every year, and require good, light ground. The stems grow to eight or ten feet high, and have the appearance of the Sunflower. They are in use from October to April. Any time in November, a quantity may be lifted and packed away in sand or earth, for Winter use; or cover the ground with rough litter, to keep out severe frost, and they can be lifted as required. The frost does not injure the tubers.

KALE (BORECOLE) — *Brassica oleracea acephala, 1894* — This vegetable of the cabbage family is grown and used in various ways, most usually as "sprouts" for winter greens, similar to spinach or collards. Sow seed in early autumn, having drills one foot apart, and leaving the plants five or six inches apart in the row. South of New York City it is hardy enough to endure the winters without protection. In spring the plants are cut, dead leaves trimmed off and used for greens. The Germans usually plant kale as one would late cabbages. Seed is sown in spring, and the plants set out in June or July, in rows three feet apart, with two or three feet distance between the plants. Same cultivation is given as for cabbages. During early winter the leaves, which grow to a considerable size, are gathered frequently when frozen, or to be dug from under the snow, and used for greens. If properly prepared they are exceedingly palatable, especially as they come at a time when fresh green stuff is quite scarce. The young sprouts issuing in spring from the stumps are also utilized for greens; and when boiled and served with vinegar, make a very popular and palatable salad.

KOHL-RABI — *Brassica Caulo-rapa, 1894* — In this we have another vegetable much less cultivated in American gardens than it deserves. As easily grown as any member of the cabbage family, it yields in its swollen, fleshy stem a most palatable dish, which combines the cabbage and turnip flavors, but in a more refined degree. It is deliciously tender, especially when used just when fully grown; but when old, becomes hard, tough and unfit for the table. The usual method of culture is to sow seed in drills, 15 or 18 inches apart, and thin to 6 or 8 inches in the row. The time for sowing is from early spring until summer, so that a succession may be had from early summer until winter. Keep the ground loose and free from weeds. With careful handling, kohl-rabi can also be transplanted successfully.

LAMBS' LETTUCE — See Corn Salad

LEAF BEET (SPINACH BEET, SWISS CHARD) —
Beta cycla, 1881 — During the season of spinach one need look for nothing better in the shape of "greens;" but when the long hot days come, these plants soon run up to seed, and it is difficult to secure a supply. Among the several plants used to furnish midsummer greens is the Leaf Beet.

It produces an abundance of leaves, having very large and thick leaf-stalks; these, when the plant is grown rapidly, are tender, and furnish an abundant supply of greens. Its culture is the same as for the ordinary beet, except to give the plants more room. In rich soil one foot apart in the rows is none too much. Sown very early, the plants will be of a full size by midsummer. The seed is sometimes sown in September, and the plants wintered with a slight covering, to give an early crop in spring. The outer leaves are pulled away, the same as in gathering rhubarb, leaving those in the center to increase and continue the supply. In this country the leaves are cooked in the same manner as other greens. In Europe the plant is expecially valued for the very broad and thick leaf stalks, which are peeled, cooked, and served in the same manner as asparagus, with drawn butter. The plant is often called "Swiss Chard," and is one of the few plants the traveller sees in the little gardens of the chalets in the mountains of Switzerland.

LEEKS — *Allium Porrum, 1864* — Those who do not like onions will not cultivate leeks, as they have a flavor resembling that of the onion, though quite peculiar. Leeks are so highly prized by the Welsh that they are as much a national vegetable for them as the potato is to the Irish. The leek differs from the onion in having broad flat leaves, and in not swelling out at the bottom. The eatable portion consists of the lower part of the leaves forming a neck which is blanched by earthing up to exclude the light. The engraving shows the appearance of the leek. Sow seed in early

spring in a light rich soil. It may be sown thinly in drills, 15 inches apart, where the plants are to stand; in this case they are thinned out to six inches in the rows, and are gradually earthed up at the summer hoeings. Some cultivators sow the seed broadcast or in drills, and when the plants are four to six inches high, they are transplanted to trenches about six inches deep, and gradually earthed up as they grow. We have found these methods equally successful. It is said that occasionally shortening the leaves will increase the size of the leek. We have never tried it. One ounce of seed will produce about two thousand plants. The leek is quite hardy and in most localities may be left out over winter, and will come out in spring "as green as a leek." Leeks are used in soups and stews. When cut up in soups and thoroughly cooked, they impart besides their peculiar flavor, a mucilaginous quality much liked by many.

LETTUCE — *Lactuca Sativa, 1894* — People who know lettuce only as loose leaves (cut-lettuce, leaf-lettuce) grown in close rows or masses, as usually found in American Kitchen gardens, have not yet learned to appreciate the possibilities of this vegetable as salad material, nor all its inherent virtues. My method of growing it for home use brings out all its best points.

At the earliest possible date in spring I sow seed of various varieties in drills 12 to 15 inches apart, and give clean and thorough cultivation from the start by means of the hand wheel-hoe, same as all the other closely planted vegetables in the patch.

Strict attention is given to early thinning, the most vigorous plants being left, so they stand about 3 or 4 inches apart in the drills. Rapid growth is forced by occasional light dressings of nitrate of soda (a little saltpetre will give similar results); and as soon as the heads have fairly begun to form, we commence using them for the table, thinning the plants as we go along, until they stand 10 or 12 inches apart in the rows. By this time they have developed into large heads, sometimes of mammoth size, and of the delicious crispness and tenderness which only rapid growth can give us. Thus we have always the very best quality of salad, the little partly-developed heads at first, and later the hard, solid, large ones. As we always have it in great abundance, the crisp inner hearts alone are used, and the large outer leaves go to the fowls. Thus grown, lettuce makes a most excellent salad, indeed, above all comparison with the stuff usually found in the markets, or in most people's kitchen garden.

In favored localities in the middle states, and almost everywhere further south, lettuce sown or planted out in open ground in the autumn will usually winter all right, especially if protected (when thought necessary) by lightly covering with evergreen boughs, or coarse litter, and will give a crop much in advance of that planted out in spring. It could go without saying that the stimulus given to plant growth by free use of the hoes cannot be safely dispensed with in the lettuce patch.

LIMA BEANS — *Phaseolus lunatus, 1863* — Few products of the garden are more acceptable than Lima beans, cooked green, and also when ripe. For some reason many persons fail in growing them well, however, They either do not come up at all, or they make a weak or sickly growth. If planted like the smaller varieties, with one to three inches of earth over them, and this perhaps packed down with the hoe and by rains, the cotyledons or seed-leaves can not force their way to the surface, and they rot. The soil should be dry, loose and warm, and the covering very light——hardly more than just to hide them. It is best to raise hills of moderate hight, and set poles before planting; then stick the beans in with the eye down, and leave them at or just below the surface. A very good plan is, to prepare a small bed of light, warm soil, on the south side of a tight fence, and stick in the beans all over its surface, two inches or so a part, and sprinkle on a very light covering of sand, or fine soil. If needed, a sprinkling of water may be given often enough to keep the soil damp. If a chance cold night occurs, throw an old blanket or mat over the bed. When sprouted, before rooting, transfer to hills. A still better way, perhaps, is to start the separate beans in bits of soil, and transfer these to the hills.

MARTYNIA — *Martynia Proboscidea, 1887* — The unripe pods, when perfectly tender, are used for pickling. They must be gathered every day or two, or some will become hard and useless. Sow in open ground in May, in drills two feet apart, and thin out to one foot.

MUSK MELON (CANTALOUPE) — *Cucumis Melo, 1894* — There are few things, if any, that are a more general object of desire for the younger members of the family, or would be more painfully missed by them, than a good supply of fine melons; and I am sure no household that has once had its fill of the

fruit, in all its freshness and lusciousness as it comes directly from the garden, will ever wish to forego the pleasures of the melon patch again, even for a single season.

A rich, warm loam, more or less sandy, and plenty of good compost or fertilizers are required. New land——on the wide rotation system——is always preferable, in order to reduce the dangers from insect and disease attacks to a minimum, and nothing better could be found very easily than a young clover or old pasture lot. Plow deep, and otherwise prepare the ground well, then mark off rows from 4 to 6 feet apart each way, according to the strength of the soil, and vigor of variety to be planted. A shovelful or two of well-rotted compost is mixed with the soil at each intersection, and a large broad hill formed with the hoe.

Next drop a dozen or two of seeds scatteringly over the hill, and cover with half an inch of soil, pressing it firmly over the seed with the back of hoe. Only the three or four thriftiest plants are left in each hill; the rest must be pulled up at the first or second hoeing. Cultivate frequently and hoe afterwards, drawing fresh soil up to the plants. Guard against the attacks of the yellow-striped cucumber bug, the squash borer and other insects; and keep free from weeds. I usually pinch off the ends of leading shoots when they have grown several feet in length, for the purpose of forcing out the laterals, on which the fruit is always borne. In early September I also remove the later settings of fruit, which cannot be expected to come to maturity before frost. In order to make the crop earlier, and at the same time protect the plants from bug attacks, they are frequently started on pieces of inverted sod, in hot-bed or cold-frame, in the same way as described for Lima beans. Care should be taken to make the transfer from frame to open ground on moist, cloudy days only; then cultivate same as directed for plants started in open ground.

NEW ZEALAND SPINACH — *Tetragonia expansa, 1847* — The great advantage this Spinach possesses over the other is that of supplying a crop of leaves in the dryest weather, when crops of other sorts have failed. From its rapidity of growth, a few dozen of plants will afford a supply during its growing season. If a few leaves of Sorrel are boiled with it, the flavor is improved.

It is a spreading, towering plant, growing in a circular form, attaining the height of four or five feet.

Sow the seed very thinly, in rows one inch deep and two feet apart, about the first week of April, in an open, rich piece of ground. Hoe freely and keep clean of weeds. The seeds, in a green state, make an excellent pickle, for which alone it is worth cultivation.

NASTURTIUM (INDIAN CRESS) — *Tropaeolum majus, 1887* — A highly ornamental plant, cultivated in flower gardens as well in the kitchen garden. The shoots and flowers are sometimes used in salads, but it is mainly grown for its fruit or seed pods, which are pickled in vinegar and used as a substitute for capers. The plant is of the easiest culture. Sow in shallow drills in May. The tall variety will reach a hight of ten or fifteen feet if furnished with strings or wires, and makes an excellent screen for shade, or for quickly covering up and concealing any unsightly place. The dwarf variety is grown like Peas, and staked with brush, or grown on the garden trellis.

OKRA (GUMBO) — *Hibiscus esculentus, 1864* — This garden vegetable is little known, but it is one which most people soon become very fond of when they use it. It is an annual, growing from two to six feet high, with rather coarse leaves, and light yellow flowers having a dark center. The plant belongs to the same family as the hollyhock and cotton, and the flowers of all three bear a strong resemblance. The young pods are the eatable portion. They are from four to eight inches long, and about an inch in diameter, angled, or several sided and tapering toward the upper end. These when tender are very mucilaginous, and are used for thickening soups and stews. The dish called gumbo at the South, consists of chicken stewed with these pods; and the same name is sometimes applied to the plant itself. The pods boiled in water and dressed with drawn butter, after the manner of asparagus, are much liked by many. Being of southern origin it requires a long season, but lately a dwarf and early variety has been introduced, which is adapted to northern climates. One ounce of seed will sow one hundred feet of row. It should be sown when the ground becomes warm, in rich soil, in drills three feet apart, and the plants should be thinned to one foot in the row. During the summer the plants should be kept clean of weeds and be slightly hilled up in hoeing. The pods are cut when nearly grown, but still tender. The green pods are sliced and dried for winter use. The ripe seeds are among the many things which have used as substitutes for coffee.

ONION — *Allium cepa, 1887* — Onions are raised either from "sets," which are small dry Onions grown the previous year, or from seeds. When grown from the sets, they should be planted out as early in spring as the ground is dry enough to work. Plant them in rows one foot apart, with the sets three or four inches apart. When raised from sets, the Onions can be used in the green state in June, or they will be ripened off by July. When raised from seeds, these are sown at about the same distance between the rows, and when the young plants are an inch or so high, they are thinned out to two or three inches apart. It is important that Onion seed be sown very early. It should be sown not later than the middle of April; for, if delayed until May, warm weather sets in and delays, or rather prolongs the growth until fall, and often the bulbs will not ripen. We find that, unless the Onion tops dry off and the bulbs ripen by August, they will hardly do so later.

OYSTER PLANT — See Salsify

PARSLEY — *Apium Petroselinum, 1888* — This should be grown by every gardener on account of its usefulness, both for seasoning and garnishing. As it seeds in the second season, fresh plantings should be made every Spring. The seed, being very slow to germinate, should be soaked in tepid water for twenty-four hours before planting. The best way is to sow in the hotbed or cold frame and transplant to the garden, but it can be sown in drills where wanted and thinned out to the proper distance apart. I always try to have a bed of it near the kitchen door, as it saves much running; if such a bed cannot be conveniently placed, some should be cut and brought in with the other vegetables, as it will keep fresh some days if kept in cold water. In the fall some of the best roots should be taken up and planted in the cold frame, or put in pots and boxes in the sunny windows of the house, for a winter supply.

PARSNEP (PARSNIP) — *Pastinaca Sativa, 1888* — This is a winter vegetable, needing hard freezing to refine and bring out its best quality; the roots should be left to stand where grown until they can be dug in the spring or through the winter as wanted, though some may be dug and stored in heaps for use when the ground is frozen too solidly to admit of digging them. If there is more than are wanted for table use, there should be no delay in getting them dug as early in the spring as possible, for when they begin to sprout and grow, they very soon become woody and unfit to eat. A row should be sown in the garden at the same time as the onions, beets, etc., are planted. It is best to sow the seed quite thickly; by thickly I mean one seed every inch or so; when the young plants are about three inches high they should be thinned out to six inches apart in the row, care being taken to leave only one plant in a place, as, if two are left, they will spoil the symmetrical shape of the roots by growing against each other. On planting the seed I always try to run it in between two rows of beets, onions, lettuce, or other early crop, thus working it with the wheel hoe while small, and when the other crops have been taken off there is room to work it with the cultivator, which is run as close to the rows and as deeply as possible, so that the roots may attain the largest size. In digging the roots when the ground is frozen hard and is impenetrable to the spade, I use a long iron post digger with a steel blade.

PEANUT (GROUND PEA) — *Arachis hypogaea, 1894* — While interesting everywhere, it is very unreliable north of Philadelphia, as it requires a long season to bring it to maturity. In the northern home garden it will especially interest the young people, and the newly introduced "Spanish" or "Improved" nut should be tried just on this account where the common Virginia peanut cannot be expected to ripen. Select warm soil, if possible of a calcareous nature; mark out rows 3 feet apart, and drop the nuts about a foot apart in the rows, one in a place, and cover with 2 inches of soil. It is not necessary to remove the hulls or shucks before planting. Cultivate and hoe freely, leaving but one plant in a place; and keep the soil well mellowed up around the plants when seeds (nuts) are forming. It is quite interesting to observe the flowers as they insert their ovaries into the mellow soil, where they complete their growth and form nuts. Before freezing weather the plants are dug, or pulled up. Hang under a shed to cure; then gather, clean and sort the nuts.

PEAS — *Pisum sativum, 1894* — I found no garden crop that I can grow with greater ease and certainty merely by a moderate application of some good complete fertilizer. Peas do best in the fore-part of the season, and should be planted early, as those planted late for "succession" hardly ever turn out very satisfactory. Sow in drills, 2 to 3 inches deep, and 2½ to 3½ feet apart, according to vigor of variety and strength of soil.

For the home garden I prefer to sow the best

would probably be the most satisfactory way to grow them, as the tall growing corn, of which there should be at least five rows between them and any other vines, would prevent the pollen from mixing, and as the hills need only be four or five feet apart, a great many could be raised in a row. The pumpkins must all be gathered in and stored before any heavy frosts, as it will spoil and start them to rotting.

RADISH — *Raphanus sativus, 1887* — One of the first vegetables that we crave in spring is the Radish, and it is so easy of culture that every family can have it fresh, crisp, and in abundance. A garden patch of a few feet square will give enough for an ordinary family, It is sown either in drills or broadcast, care being taken that the seed is not put in too thickly; from one to two inches apart, either in drill or broadcast, being the proper distance, as usually every seed germinates.

RHUBARB (PIE-PLANT) — *Rheum rhaponticum, 1888* — Rhubarb, known familiarly as Pie Plant, succeeds best in deep, somewhat retentive soil. Coming, as it does, before berries or fruit, its acid leaf stalks form an admirable substitute. It may be raised from seed, but to get the quickest returns procure strong roots in spring, and plant them three feet apart each way, the ground having first been fertilized and dug to a considerable depth. Never permit a plant to exhaust itself by seed-bearing; stir the soil often, cover with coarse litter in fall, fork it over in the following spring, and you may rely upon a good supply of pie plant for many years to come.

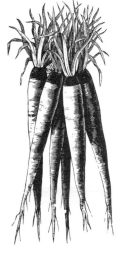

SALSIFY (OYSTER PLANT) — *Tragopogon porri-folius, 1882* — The Salsify, or Vegetable Oyster, is one of the choicest of our family vegetables, considered as a luxury. It may not furnish as nutritious food as some other kinds, but of this I am not certain, though I am certain that if it were better known it would be more cultivated. The root resembles the Parsnip, but its flavor is much like that of the oyster, hence the popular name, Oyster Plant. There is no more trouble in growing this choice vegetable than Carrots; indeed, about the same treatment is needed. I like to sow early, because the seed germinates slowly, and in a deep, light soil, because then I get longer, straighter roots. I sow the seed in drills, from twelve to fifteen inches apart, and cover it not much more than an inch in depth; when the plants appear, thin to four or five inches apart in the rows. In September we begin their use, and continue to take them from the garden as needed until winter appears to be setting in, when a quantity are stored in a cool cellar, and covered with earth, for winter use. A portion remain in the ground for spring consumption, and we use them from the garden until they begin to go to seed, which will be some time in May. The roots are simply boiled, like Beets and Carrots, but sliced up and made into a soup they are delicious.

SCORZONERA (BLACK SALSIFY) — *Scorzonera Hispanica, 1894* — A perennial, cultivated either as annual or biennial, exactly like Salsify, with this difference that the roots, if left in the ground, will continue to grow in size and to remain fit for use. Use like salsify.

SEA KALE — *Crambe maritima, 1850* — The flavor is more delicate to my taste than asparagus, and as it has the merit of being more of a novelty, the gardener should always have a bed of it. It wants deep, rich soil, like asparagus, and beds made in the same way, answer well for sea kale. Sandy soil is the most congenial to it. To make beds of sea kale, sow the seeds in April, and thin them out, when well growing, so as to leave them about twelve inches apart. In the autumn cover the beds with a little manure, and over this spread three or four inches of black bog earth that has been well pulverized; or, if you have it at hand, tan bark will answer equally as well—charcoal dust is still better. Through this layer, the young shoots will rise in the spring, and force their way up in a blanched state. They are then ready for cutting and cooking, as the sea kale, like celery, must be blanched. When you have cut over the bed twice, remove the loose materials, except the manure, which, (with the addition of a slight sprinkling of refuse salt,) may be lightly turned under. The plants then grow all summer, and at the end of autumn the blanch covering should be again renewed. Considering how much importance every body seems to attach to the asparagus bed, it is surprising how little sea kale is known. I am sure if one half the ground usually devoted to asparagus, were occupied by a permanent bed of sea kale, it would give more variety, and more satisfaction, at the dinner table.

SHALLOTS — *Allium ascalonicum, 1887* — A plant of the Onion genus, which is cultivated by setting out the divided bulbs in September in rows a foot apart, allowing six inches between them. It is entirely hardy, and fit for use in early spring.

SKIRRET — *Sium Sisarum, 1857* — Skirret is considered a nutricious vegetable, and would be more generally cultivated were it not for the large space of ground required to raise a quantity for general use. It is a perennial plant, a native of Asia, and has been cultivated in Europe about two hundred years. The roots are composed of long, fleshy tubers, joined together in the crown or head. They are cooked like Salsafy, and form a very white, sweet, and pleasant vegetable.

Soil suitable for the Carrot will also grow this root in perfection. Sow the seeds thinly, in drills, half an inch deep and ten inches wide, at any time from the middle of April to the first of May, the ground having been previously well dug and manured. Sow a few Radish seeds in the drills, to distinguish them, and admit of hoeing to destroy the weeds, lest they overgrow the crop. In five or six weeks they can be thinned out with the hoe to five or six inches apart. Nothing more will be requisite, excepting a constant stirring of the soil and keeping down weeds. About the first of November the roots will be fit for use, and continue so till Spring. On the approach of severe frost, they should be taken up, cleaned and stowed away, like other roots, in sand or dry earth.

SORREL (BROAD-LEAFED SORREL) — *Rumex Actosa, 1894* — Used to a limited extent for soups and salads. Usually grown from seed, which is sown in early spring in good soil, having rows one foot apart. Thin the plants to stand five or six inches apart in the rows. The leaves are the part used. Cut out the seed-stalk, as soon as it appears.

SPINACH (SPINAGE) — *Spinacia oleracea, 1888* — This is a quick-growing green, and very hardy, making it valuable for early spring and late fall growing. It cannot be raised during summer, on account of its running immediately to seed without making many leaves. It can be sown as soon as the ground can be worked in the spring, and will be ready for use in a few weeks; about three sowings may be made, two weeks apart, or more, if the season is longer, though it will hardly be good if planted after the middle of May. The whole plant is cut off even with the ground, at any time before it starts to run to seed, the leaves and stems being used as boiled greens. Large sowings should be made in October, of the hardy variety, as it can be cut throughout the winter; a later sowing may be made the first of November, and lightly covered with litter when the ground has been frozen hard; this covering should be raked off early in the spring, and it will complete its growth before the first spring planting is ready for use.

SPINACH BEET — See Leaf Beet

SQUASH — *Cucurbita Pepo, 1887* — As with all plants of this class, it is useless to sow the seeds before warm weather in May, and the directions given for Cucumbers and Melons are alike applicable to the Squash, except the distances apart of the hills, which should be from three to four feet for the bush sorts, and from six to eight for the other varieties, which "run" or make a long vine. The fall or winter Squashes are planted at the same time, but are allowed to mature or ripen, while the summer varieties are used green. They are usually planted eight or nine feet apart, in hills prepared in the usual way. These Squashes are great feeders, and for the best results the soil should be well enriched, besides the special manuring in the hills, as the vines throw out roots at every joint to assist in feeding and maturing the heavy crop they usually bear.

SUCCORY — See Chicory

SWEET POTATO — *Ipomaea Batatas, 1887* — It is useless to attempt to grow the Sweet Potato on anything but a light and dry soil. On clayey soils the plant not only grows poorly, but the potatoes raised upon such soil are watery and poorly flavored. The plants are raised by laying the roots on their sides on a hot-bed or the bench of a greenhouse, and covering them over with sand, about the first week in May. By keeping up an average temperature of seventy-five or eighty degrees, fine plants will be produced by June 1st, at which time they should be planted. The plants are set in hills three feet apart each way, or on ridges four feet apart, and twelve or fifteen inches between the plants, drawing the earth up to them as they grow, until the top of the ridge or hill is four or six inches above the level. The soil under the ridges should be highly manured, and as the vines grow they should be kept clear of weeds. When, late in the season, they show a disposition to root at the joints, they must be moved every week or so. This is easily done by running a rake handle or other stick under the vines, and lifting them sufficiently to draw out the small roots upon the stem. As is the case with many other vegetables of which the plants or sets are raised in large quantities for sale, it is better and

cheaper, when Sweet Potato plants are procurable, to purchase them, than to attempt to raise the small number required in a private garden.

SWISS CHARD — See Leaf Beet

TOMATO — *Lycopersicum esculentum, 1888* — The seed is sown in hotbeds, from the middle of March to the middle of April; if possible, they should be transplanted, when about two inches high, to another sash, where they may stand three or four inches apart. When there is not room for this, the seed should be sown thinly in drills four inches apart, and when well started, should be thinned out to two inches apart in the row. The hotbeds should be given plenty of air on warm days that the plants may be stocky and thrifty when planting-time comes. They should not be set out until the temperature is over 60° at night, or until the oak trees are well out in leaf. They should have plenty of room, at least three feet in the row and four feet between the rows.

The young plants must be thoroughly cultivated and hoed; when hoeing, the dirt should be loosened right up to the plant, and when it has been worked loose and made fine should be drawn up to the stem, two or three inches in height.

The earliest hotbed plants will begin to ripen fruit the last week in July or the first in August, while, if you make a hill, as for corn, about May 10th, and put in in a dozen or so seed where you want the plant to stand, pulling all out but the strongest one when they get a good start, you can have this second lot in bearing about the last of August, without the use of glass or the labor of transplanting.

The ground should be well manured, but if the soil is light it can be overdone, as the plant will run too much to vine and be late in producing fruit.

TURNIP ROOTED CHERVIL — *Chaerophyllum bulbosa, 1894* — The root of this hardy vegetable resembles a short carrot or parsnip; somewhat smaller, of dark gray color, and with yellowish white flesh, which is sweet and mealy, reminding of sweet potato. Chervil, if fresh seed is sown, either in autumn or early spring, is of easy culture, being managed and used in same way as parsnips. It succeeds everywhere, and is improved by frost. The stalks grow tall and vigorous, and die down early in the season, indicating that the tubers have reached maturity.

TURNIPS — *Brassica campestris, 1888* — With our hot, dry summers, turnips can only be raised satisfactorily as a fall crop. They can be grown as a second crop, after early sweet corn, potatoes or peas, and should be sown as soon as possible after the first of August. The ground should be plowed or run over two or three times with the cultivator, and then harrowed till it is as fine as it is possible to make it. If the seed is sown broadcast, some winter radish seed should be mixed and sown with it. The ground should be rolled after sowing, not only to compact the soil round the seeds, which is essential to good germination, but also to prevent washing by the September rains, if the ground is at all sloping. But where the finest turnips and a sure crop are desired, it is much better to sow our garden turnips in drills, one foot apart if you have a wheel hoe, or as narrow as you cultivate, if you have not. This will tend to having the roots of even size, and the finest appearance, as they can be frequently worked. When about three inches high, or when beginning to form bulbs, they should be thinned out to four or five inches apart in the rows, with the narrow hoe, leaving each bulb to stand by itself. It will be found that by this method, with careful culture, a larger as well as a much finer crop can be raised on the ground than if they were sown broadcast, and that not half as much seed need be used, as it is carefully planted just where it is to grow.

About the third week in November, or before there is danger of the ground becoming hard, the turnips should be pulled and the tops cut off; take enough in the cellar for immediate use, and store the rest in heaps.

UPLAND CRESS (AMERICAN CRESS) — *Barbarea praecox, 1894* — Native biennial of Europe, resembling Water Cress in taste, and used for seasoning and garnishing. Easily grown from seed. I have no high opinion of it, and do not recommend it.

VEGETABLE MARROW — *Cucurbita ovifera, 1847* — We have been frequently greatly amused by some of our friends kindly presenting us with seeds purporting to be the marrow of all the vegetables, or "Vegetable Marrow." It is a species of Gourd introduced from Persia several years ago, and has been found useful for culinary purposes in every stage of its growth. When young, it is cut in slices and fried with butter; when more mature, it is cut in quarters, stewed in rich gravy, and seasoned to taste; in this

way it is very agreeable, and said to be both wholesome and nutritious.

This vegetable is characteristically situated between the Pumpkin and the Squash, consequently its habits and mode of growth are very similar to those plants. Plant the seeds in hills, about the first of May, six feet apart, and manage them as directed for the above. It has an oval fruit inside, very fleshy. In saving the seed, keep the plants distant from any of the family.

VITTICOST — See Corn Salad

WATER CRESS — *Nasturtium officinale, 1887* — A hardy aquatic plant, which can only be properly cultivated where there are running streams. If there is a brook on the place, all that would be wanted for private use may be had by setting a few plants or sowing seeds in spring on the margin of the water. There is a variety recently introduced known as "Upland Cress," that can be grown in an ordinary garden. It is almost identical in flavor with the Water Cress.

WATER MELON — *Citrullus vulgaris, 1887* — The cultivation of the Water Melon is in all respects similar to that of the Musk Melon, except that, being a larger and stronger growing plant, it requires to be planted at greater distances. The hills should not be less than eight feet apart each way. It delights in a light, sandy soil, and will not grow satisfactorily on heavy, clayey soils.

Hints on
Planting, Protecting & Growing
Your Garden

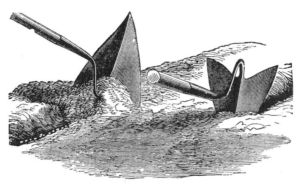

◆ ◆ ◆

Starting Seedlings

Where a sunny kitchen window is at disposal for the purpose, some tomato, pepper and egg-plants can easily be started in a box or in boxes placed in front of it, as shown in illustration. Suitable soil is prepared by mixing one-third of well-rotted compost and two-thirds sandy loam or rich garden soil, and of course it should be got in readiness in the autumn before the ground freezes. The boxes are filled with this nearly to the top, and the seeds sowed thinly in shallow furrows. Each variety should be plainly labelled, or the name written on outside of box facing each row. Sift a little sandy loam, leaf mould or pulverized dried peat moss upon the seeds, pat it down gently to firm the seed, then water with hot water from a fine rose sprinkler, and as often afterwards with tepid water as the soil becomes dry, and needs it. Thus treated the young plants should make their appearance in about a week's time. A few cabbage, cauliflower and lettuce plants may be grown in a similar way, but the box should be set in a colder room, or in a less sunny exposure. The chief aim must be to make the plants strong and stocky by giving each sufficient space, and thin out the surplus at an early stage of development. Tall, over-grown things are not desirable.

From the 1894 book, HOW TO MAKE THE GARDEN PAY

The "Tomato Egg-Plant" from Johnson & Stokes' 1889 seed catalog

• • •

I know of nothing so interesting as watching the growth and development of some new and improved variety that has been recommended to the gardening public in the most glowing terms, and often in flowing colors on a beautiful colored plate. Although I have been "taken in" fully as often as the average gardener of my experience, I have been many times repaid all trouble and outlay by the numerous successes that I have met with and the great improvement in some of the varieties grown. Sometimes I have made quite a nice little sum out of these novelties, when I have been able to sell the selected seed of the variety to some other seedsman or to my neighbors. In these new varieties, more than in any others, do you need to order early, or, instead of the seed that you desire and which is to make reputation and money for you, "being something superior to anything ever grown before," you may get one of those provoking little slips stating that the seedsman "regrets to inform you that, owing to the great demand, the supply is exhausted for this season, and hopes that the substituted kind will do as well."

From the 1888 book, HOW AND WHAT TO GROW IN A KITCHEN GARDEN OF ONE ACRE

How to Prepare Your Beds

As the truth of the old adage, that one ounce of prevention is of more value than a pound of cure, is very generally admitted, I would recommend the following method of preparing a bed for the purpose of raising Cabbage, Cauliflower, Broccoli, and such other plants as are subject to the attacks of insects: After digging or ploughing the ground in the usual way, collect any combustibles that are attainable, as dried weeds, sedge, turf, brushwood, leaves, stubble, corn-stalks, sawdust, or even litter from the dung-heap, which should be placed in heaps on the seed-beds and burned to ashes; then rake the ground over and sow the seed, which will not be attacked by insects while the effects of the fire remain. In the event of extremely dry weather, water the beds every evening until the plants are in full leaf. This is an infallible remedy.

Worms, maggots, snails, or slugs, may be driven away by sowing salt or lime in the spring, in the proportion of two to three bushels per acre, or by watering the soil occasionally with salt and water, using about two pounds of salt to four gallons of water; or the slug kind may be easily entrapped on small beds of plants, by strewing slices of turnip on them late in the evening, on which the slug or snail will readily crowd, and may be gathered up early in the morning (before sunrise) and destroyed.

From the 1866 book, THE AMERICAN GARDENER'S ASSISTANT

How Wide Should Your Garden Rows Be?

In planting the rows in the spring, the width of the cultivator must be taken into account. If the ground has been heavily manured the vegetables can be planted as closely as will admit of working, and allowing a good supply of light and air to the roots, excepting melons and other vines, which should have plenty of room in which to spread and sun themselves.

From the 1888 book, HOW AND WHAT TO GROW IN A KITCHEN GARDEN OF ONE ACRE

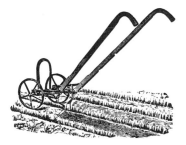

How to Sow

From the 1894 book, HOW TO MAKE THE GARDEN PAY

For the home garden, and where only small quantities of any one variety are planted, as in test plats for instance, the use of the drill is hardly desirable, and hand sowing is far preferable. A little practice will enable any one of average skill to make a clean job of it. The rows are marked out with the garden marker, and the operator, taking the seed paper in left hand, walks along the row and drops the seed evenly from the right hand held in the position shown in picture. The little finger and its neighbor form a sort of receptacle for a quantity of seed which gradually works down, and is evenly dropped by the other three fingers, through a rubbing motion of the thumb against the next two fingers. A person can easily learn to sow in this way nearly as evenly and uniformly as is done by the use of the drill.

The covering is done by simply drawing a steel rake lengthwise over each row, and the firming either by the use of the feet, or by patting with the back of the rake. My favorite practice is to rake in the seed of the first row, then while plying the rake over the second row, to walk on the first row, thus firming it, next, while covering the third row, to walk on the second, etc. Covering and firming all at one time, can also be done without rake, and by the use of the feet alone.

Some of the very fine seeds, like celery, need particularly careful handling. The drill marks are made very shallow, the seed sown rather thickly, and the soil merely firmed by the use of the feet, or back of rake. Special devices are sometimes used for very small seeds, such as covering the soil after seed is sown and lightly covered, with a pane of glass or piece of cloth, etc., and this left on until the young plants appear above ground.

Covering Your Seed

Gardeners practise different methods of covering up seed; some do it with a hoe, others with a rake or harrow; some draw a portion of the earth to the side of the bed, and after sowing the seed, return it regularly over the bed; in some particular cases a sieve is used, in others a roller. Rolling or treading in seed is necessary in dry seasons; but it should never be done when the ground is wet.

Many kinds of seed, such as Asparagus, Capsicum, Celery, Fetticus, Leek, Lettuce, Onion, Parsnip, Parsley, Rhubarb, Salsify, Spinach, etc., will not vegetate freely in dry weather unless the ground be watered or rolled. Where there is no roller on the premises, the following contrivance may answer for small beds as a substitute: after seed is sown, and the ground well raked, take a board the whole length of the bed, lay it flat on the ground, begin at one edge of the bed, and walk the whole length of it; this will press the soil on the seed; then shift the board till you have gone over the whole bed. In the absence of boards, tread in the seed with your feet, or strike on the bed with the back of your spade or shovel; but this should not be done when the ground is wet.

By Thomas Bridgeman, from his 1866 book, THE AMERI-CAN GARDENER'S ASSISTANT

Firm Your Soil

In sowing all kinds of seeds, more particularly those of small size, be careful, if the soil is dry, to "firm" or press down the surface of the bed or row, after sowing, with the feet, or a light roller, or the back of a spade, more especially if the weather is beginning to get warm. Crops are often lost through the failure of the seeds to germinate, for the simple reason that the soil is left loose about the tiny seeds, and the dry atmosphere penetrates to them, shriveling them up until all vitality is destroyed. We sow nearly all vegetable crops in rows, and in every case, as soon as the seed is sown, it is pressed down in the drill with the foot, then covered up level by the back of a rake drawn lengthways with the drills, and again firmed by the roller or back of a spade. For want of this simple precaution, perhaps one-fourth of all seeds sown fail to germinate, and the seedsman is blamed, while the fault is owing entirely to the ignorance or carelessness of the planter. Again, for the same reason, when setting out plants of any kind, be certain that the soil is pressed close to the root. In our large plantings in market gardening, particularly in summer, we make it a rule in dry weather to turn back on the row after planting it with the dibber or trowel, and press the earth firmly to each plant with the foot. We have seen whole acres of Celery, Cabbage, and Strawberry plants lost solely through neglect of this precaution.

By Peter Henderson, from his 1887 book, GARDENING FOR PLEASURE

Hints on Setting·out Seedlings

Inexperienced gardeners are apt to think that a rainy day is the only fit time for setting out plants, and will often delay a week or two longer than is necessary waiting for it, and finally plant when the ground is soaked and when they sink to their ankles in the soil. That is the worst time that could possibly be chosen, excepting when the ground is congealed with cold. For it is impossible that the mold, sticky and clammy while wet, can filter among the roots, or remain of suitable texture for them to spread themselves in, permeable to them and equally pervious to the air in every part without anywhere exposing their tender parts to actual contact in chambers of corrosive oxygen. A rainy day is an advantage if the plants are set before the ground has become wet, but the safe and sure way is to go for the plants as soon as the ground is fully prepared, no matter how dry the weather. A pail or bucket should always be taken to carry the plants in, having a little water in the bottom. The roots being set in this will absorb until the plant is so gorged that it will endure a drying air after being set in place. If the ground is very dry, water should be poured in before planting, which is very much better than pouring upon the surface, because of no injurious crust being formed, for a continually open surface during the growing season, to admit of free circulation of air and capillary action from below, is absolutely essential to free profitable growth.

From THE NATIONAL FARMER'S AND HOUSE-KEEPER'S CYCLOPAEDIA, 1888

♦ ♦ ♦ ♦ ♦

Should an unusually early and warm spring induce you to plant more largely before the usual time, one precaution must never be lost sight of, namely, to hold a supply of good plants in reserve for the very possible emergency of a mishap to those set out first. Here is just where so many growers come to grief annually, and almost every year we see people, after having lost their plants by a late frost, anxiously hunting the country over in June, for a new supply, and finally being compelled to take up with a poor lot of late grown plants, or go without.

From the 1894 book, HOW TO MAKE THE GARDEN PAY

♦ ♦ ♦ ♦ ♦

It is desirable in transplanting not to check the growth by disturbing the roots. A good way to avoid this is to scrape out turnips, fill them with good soil and plant in two or three seeds, setting them in a warm, light place, and keeping them moist. When the weather is suitable, place these out in the garden at the proper depth. The turnip will decay and the plant will thrive unchecked if properly cared for. Do not use potatoes instead of turnips. Another method is to get squares of sod, say six inches wide, from good, mellow soil, turn them bottom up, and put such seeds as squash, melon or sweet corn, and treat them in the same way, not putting out till the weather is quite warm, and then protecting against bugs. For more delicate plants, flowers, etc., make little square paper boxes out of thin writing paper, or thick newspaper, merely folding them at the corners as you would the paper in covering a book, and tacking them with a needle and thread; make them about three inches square and two deep. Fill with good soil; start the seeds and put them out at the proper time, boxes and all, without disturbing the roots. If you fear the paper is too strong for the roots to penetrate, cut carefully on the bottom of the box the shape of a cross, and all will be well.

From THE NATIONAL FARMER'S AND HOUSE-KEEPER'S CYCLOPAEDIA, 1888

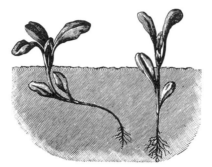

Spindling Plants.—Even the most ill-looking, spindling, almost rootless plants of tomatoes, cabbages, cauliflowers, etc., can be transplanted with entire success under average conditions of soil and season. All that is needed is to insert the plants into the ground up to their very hearts. Overgrown tomato plants may be laid down in the slanting position, care being taken to bring the moist earth in firm contact with the soil where underground. Cabbages may be set either straight down or slanting, according to depth of surface soil and length of stalk. In either case roots will form all along the stems, and the heads will grow closely above the ground, instead of being held high up as if on stilts.

By T. Greiner, from his 1894 book, HOW TO MAKE THE GARDEN PAY

◆ ◆ ◆ ◆ ◆

While the cabbage, cauliflower, beets and lettuce may be planted out as soon as all danger of frost is over, the tomatoes, peppers, egg plants, etc., should not be set out until the thermometer stands at over 60° all night, or until the oak leaves are as large as a five-cent piece.

From the 1888 book, HOW AND WHAT TO GROW IN A KITCHEN GARDEN OF ONE ACRE

◆ ◆ ◆ ◆ ◆

I would call attention of you readers to a method I have long practiced in starting Lima Beans, Melons, and Cucumbers early. It is not new, but I know very few who have adopted it, and it may prove of service to some one this spring. With a sharp spade I cut some pieces of turf, from a rich soil, in pieces about four inches square and three inches thick; these I place bottom side up in a cold frame, and in each stick two Beans or Melon seeds and cover lightly with soil. The young plants soon appear and advance rapidly. When the weather is suitable, the pieces of turf are removed to the places the plants are to occupy. The young plants scarcely feel the shift, and valuable time is gained.

From VICK'S MONTHLY MAGAZINE, 1880

Cloudy weather permits of setting out plants safely and with equally satisfactory success at any time of day or night; but when the sun shines hot and bright, and the soil is somewhat dry, the proverbial "after 4 p. m." is the right and proper time, and better than earlier in the day. If a little shade can be provided for newly set plants, it is certainly worth some trouble to do so—soiled and discarded berry boxes, broken pots, etc., answer a good purpose, and leaves of large weeds, burdock, for instance, will be much better than nothing. Good celery plants are quite sure to survive the fiercest heat, on first being transplanted, if shaded for some days with a line of boards resting upon blocks or little stakes, and held there a few inches above ground. Bottomless plant pots (5 inch) which I had made for the purpose of bleaching celery, make first-class plant protectors, and plants thus covered for a few days, as appearing in picture, generally pass safely over the critical period. Tomatoes, egg plants and sweet potatoes, all of which rather enjoy heat, and are somewhat indifferent to drought, require less care in the selection of cloudy weather, or moist soil when planting out, and may often be set safely when cabbage and celery plants could not be transferred to the open ground without suffering considerable loss.

From the book, HOW TO MAKE THE GARDEN PAY, 1894

♦ ♦ ♦ ♦ ♦

The most tender species of plants frequently perish from excess of rain. Lima Beans, for instance, have often to be replanted three or four times in the month of May before any will stand. Melons, Cucumbers, Egg-plants, Tomato plants, etc., are sometimes cut off by variableness of the weather. Those who plant tender things in open gardens early in the season, must reconcile themselves to loss in the event of unfavorable weather, instead of throwing blame on the seeds-man.

From the 1866 book, THE AMERICAN GARDENER'S ASSISTANT

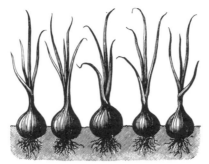

Onions properly thinned.

Thin Your Plants

The liberal use of seed gives us the desrable full stand; but also the less desirable feature of a great surplus of plants. Every plant, not required for making the crop, is practically a weed, as it deprives those that are to remain of moisture, food and room. To remove the superfluous, useless eaters and drinkers at an early period of development is just as essential as the early removal of weeds. Uniformity of vegetables——radishes, beets, onions, etc., ——and an even development cannot well be obtained except by giving each plant in the row a uniform and reasonable large amount of space. The annexed figures illustrate the contrast between a section of rows where the crop (onions) was thinned at an early stage of growth, and one where thinning is neglected. The gardener whose aim is in the direction of an early crop——of beets, radishes, etc., which he can gather all at once, clearing the rows as he goes along, and thus having them ready for a successive crop——has no other way but thin early and thoroughly. The home gardener may do this work gradually with best results. So for instance in case of table beets. Instead of thinning all at once to the generally recommended distance of 4 to 6 inches apart, the plants may at first be left 2 or 3 inches apart; and when the roots have grown of some size, and begin to crowd each other in the row, every other one be removed, giving the choicest young and tender table beets, greens, etc. A similar course can be adopted with lettuce, and people who obtain their supply of vegetables

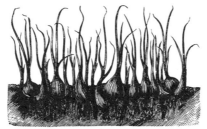

Onions left unthinned.

in the open market have no idea what luxury the small and tender hearts of half-grown lettuce afford. Try it once by thinning drilled lettuce to three or four inches apart, and when they have nicely begun to head, pulling up every other plant, and preparing just the young hearts for the table. These are some of the pleasures in the garden that mere money cannot buy.

From the book, HOW TO MAKE THE GARDEN PAY, 1894

Protect Your Seedlings from Late Frost

Some afternoon in early spring the weather reports announce the rapid approach of a cold wave, and all the indications point to a coming freeze. Then comes the anxious inquiry: How can we save our nice tomato plants, our sweet corn, potatoes and beans, all of which were growing so finely? It will not do to stand by with folded arms, complaining of the weather, and bad luck. Our only safety lies in covering the plants. This may be done by sheets of cloth or paper, litter, or by boxes, large flower pots, etc. The number of boxes and pots on hand in average gardens may not go very far, and I would advise to make use of common manilla paper bags (the sacks of grocers) for placing over tomato, and egg plants, etc. Smaller sizes will answer for pepper and smaller plants generally. Round off the corners at the open end slightly, and fasten bag to the ground by a little wooden pin thrust through each of the two flaps and into the ground, or by a small chunk of soil or a stone placed upon each flap, as may be seen in the accompanying figure.

By T. Greiner, from his 1894 book, HOW TO MAKE THE GARDEN PAY

Good Help Isn't Hard to Find

• • • • •

First of all, save and protect the birds. Almost all of them are insect-eaters, and many among them, even English sparrows, are at one time or other helping to clear the farmer's fields and gardens of insects. The young of the English sparrow are raised almost entirely on insect food. So are the young of robin "Redbreast." Grown birds feast on grasshoppers, cicadas, May-beetles, etc., whenever they have a chance, preferring this diet to other food. Crows, owls, and many hawks usually do us more good than harm. Quails, like crows, are great grub-eaters. They need protection, not persecution.

◆ ◆ ◆

Learn to know your friends among insects. The common lady bug lives largely on plant lice, eggs of potato bugs, etc. The ferocious ground beetle hunts and devours canker worms, army worms, and especially cut worms. Four-winged dragon flies feed upon mosquitoes, etc. The soldier bug and the grand lebia seem to consider the potato bug larva a dainty dish, and destroy great numbers of them. Species of spider, known familiarly as "grand-daddy-long-legs," also make themselves useful by feasting on noxious insects. Blister beetles serve to prevent excessive multiplication of grasshoppers, etc. All these useful insects deserve protection.

◆ ◆ ◆

Don't kill the toad. Its value as an insect-eater is more generally recognized in England and France than here, for the homely animal has become a regular article of trade in the markets of London and Paris. The demand for the article by English gardeners, in fact, exceeds the home supply, and dealers have begun to look to this country for additional stock. In small gardens we might often employ toads as guards around hills of choice melons, squashes, etc., by providing them with a suitable guard house or hiding place, under a piece of board, a stone, or some rubbish right among the plants. Place one or more specimens in a hotbed or cold frame, and see the insects disappear. Every crawling thing that comes within sight and reach of the toad, may its smell be ever so disgusting, its flavor ever so rank, its shell ever so hard, falls a prey to the toad's voracious appetite. The toad seems to be always ready for business.

From the 1894 book, HOW TO MAKE THE GARDEN PAY

Weeding

In no work in which men are engaged is the adage, "A stitch in time saves nine," more applicable than to the work of the garden. The instant that weeds appear, attack them with the hoe or rake. Do not wait for them to get a foot high, or a twelfth part of it, but break every inch of the surface crust of the ground just as soon as a germ of weed growth shows itself. And it will be better to do it even before any weeds show; for by using a small, sharp steel rake, two or three days after your crop is planted or sown, you will kill the weeds just as they are germinating. The newly developed germ of the strongest weed is at that time very tender. In my market garden operations I had one man whose almost exclusive duty it was to work in summer with the steel rake; and in a few days after a crop was planted the surface was raked over, destroying the thousands of weeds just ready to appear. Had we waited for the weeds to be seen, so that they were too large to be destroyed by the raking, four men could not have done with the hoe the work accomplished by this man with the rake.

From the 1887 book, GARDENING FOR PLEASURE

A Good Scare·Crow

From THE AMERICAN AGRICULTURIST, 1876

The best scare is one in which there is a constant change of motion, which confuses the memory, and bewilders the intelligence of the crow. The illustration shows such a scare, which consists of a frame mounted unpon a post and attached to a small wind-mill, by which it is kept rotating. The frame has four bars, from one to another of which wires are strung, and to the wires are fastened many pieces of bright tin, glass, both plain and colored, broken crockery, and colored feathers or rags. The rotating frame is mounted in a stationary one, and as it revolves, the bright pieces flutter and change positions at every moment, reflecting flashes of light when the sun shines, and jangling continually when the wind blows. The effectiveness of this scare-crow may be increased by hanging a few small bells upon the top bar of the outer frame, so that the clappers may be moved by the edges of the inner rotating frame as they revolve. One such scare-crow in a ten-acre field, will keep the crows at a respectful distance for the whole season, and the ingenious builder will never be humiliated by finding a sentinel crow, perching contemptuously upon the top of it, as is sometimes seen upon the outstretched arm, or the simulated gun, of the usual dummy in the corn-field, while the rest of the flock are busily engaged at their mischief in its vicinity.

How to Protect Your Crops from the Weather

The most effectual method we have found for preserving peas from withering or drying up in a drouth, is to mulch them thickly with coarse hay or straw, to a width of at least two feet on each side of the row. Our garden soil is a fine, porous gravel, and unless the season is cool and moist, the pea vines dry up so badly as to produce little fruit. Mulching heavily is consequently a necessity in order to save them. By doing this, we have obtained as good crops as when May, June, and July were cool and rather rainy. It is not necessary to bush dwarf peas. Still, when exposed to a strong wind, they will sometimes blow down, and then the further advantage of their being mulched is that the pods are kept clean and dry, and escape being mildewed. It is an excellent thing also to mulch both pole and bush beans, melons, squashes and cucumbers in the same way.

From THE AMERICAN AGRICULTURIST, 1883

◆ ◆ ◆ ◆ ◆

Covering with hay, straw, paper, muslin, etc., is about the only feasible plan of protecting crops against the first early fall frosts. The home gardener can often save a few tomato and pepper plants, melon and cucumber vines, etc., by such means, and thus prolong his season of fresh fruits of these tender garden plants for several weeks, for a warm spell usually follows closely upon the first, and (often only) early fall frost. A few tomato and pepper plants may also be lifted with all the soil that will adhere to the roots, and placed in tubs or boxes in the cellar, or under a shed; or they may be simply pulled up and hung up somewhere out of the reach of frost. They will then ripen all the larger fruit that is on them, and give a full supply some time after all the plants left in the open ground are killed by frost.

The crops of winter squashes, late melons, and all others which even the slightest touch of frost would render worthless for keeping, should of course be gathered and stored in a safe place before such mishap can befall them. Full-grown green melons, if properly stored, may be kept for some time, and yet come to full maturity.

From the 1894 book, HOW TO MAKE THE GARDEN PAY

The operation of watering before sunrise, in counteracting the frost, seems to produce its effects in a manner similar to the application of cold water to a frozen joint or limb, which is injured by the sudden application of warmth. This plan has long been adopted by the London nurserymen, when their plants have been affected by frost during the night, and is attended with the most marked success. Vegetables of any sort may be recovered by this application, and it should be attended to by the gardener, both in the spring and autumn.

From THE FARMER'S EVERY-DAY BOOK, 1851

How to Protect Your Crops from Pests

There is nothing that protects young crops of Turnips, Cabbage, and other small plants, from the depredations of the fly so well as rolling; for when the surface is rendered completely smooth, these insects are deprived of the harbor they would otherwise have under the clods and small lumps of earth. This method will be found more effectual than soaking the seed in any preparation, or dusting the plants with any composition whatever; but the roller must only be used previous to, or at the time of sowing the seed, and not when the soil is so moist that it will pack and bake, thus forming a crust on the surface of the ground, through which the young plants can never force their way.

A correspondent has communicated the result of an experiment he has tried for preventing the attacks of flies or fleas on Turnips. He says: "Steep your seed in a pint of warm water for two hours, in which is infused one ounce of saltpetre; then dry the seed, and add linseed oil sufficient to wet the whole; after which mix it with plaster of Paris, so as to separate and render it fit for sowing."

To prevent depredations from crows, steep corn in

strong saltpetre brine, sow it over the land, or steep your seed-corn; and if the crows once get a taste, they will forsake the field.

By Thomas Bridgeman, from his 1866 book, THE AMERICAN GARDENER'S ASSISTANT

◆ ◆ ◆ ◆ ◆

A spoonful of malt placed here and there, and covered by a flower pot or other dish to prevent their access to it, will prove very attractive to slugs, which will assemble around the bait during the night and may be killed in the morning. Next to malt, he has found grated carrots used in the same way to be the most attractive bait.

From THE AMERICAN AGRICULTURIST, 1867

◆ ◆ ◆ ◆ ◆

Moles may be annoyed and driven away, by obstructing the passage in their burrows with sticks smeared with tar. First insert a clean stick from the surface through the burrows; then dip others in tar, and pass them through into the floor of the burrows, being careful not to rub off the tar in the operation.

The approach of caterpillars is discoverable on the leaves of Cabbages, many of which are reduced to a thin white skin by the minute insects which emerge from the eggs placed on them. These leaves being gathered and thrown into the fire, a whole host of enemies may be destroyed at once; whereas, if they are suffered to remain, they will increase so rapidly, that in a few days the plantation, however extensive, may become infested; and, when once these arrive at the butterfly, or moth stage of existence, they become capable of perpetuating their destructive race to an almost unlimited extent.

In the summer season, Broccoli, Cabbage, Cauliflower, etc., are particularly subject to the ravages of grubs and caterpillars. To prevent this wholly, is perhaps impossible; still it is not difficult to check these troublesome visitors. It may be done by searching for them on their first appearance, and destroying them. Early in the morning, grubs may be collected from the earth, within two or three inches of such plants as they may have attacked the night previous.

Fish oil is known to be destructive to ants and various other small insects, but it is difficult to apply to plants.

From the 1866 book, THE AMERICAN GARDENER'S ASSISTANT

The young plants of late cabbages are generally infested, while in the seed bed, with a small black fly, which greatly checks their growth, and sometimes entirely destroys them. These can be gotten rid of or better, entirely avoided, by the application of dry road dust, soot, or plaster, dusted on the young leaves early in the morning, while the dew is still on them; this should be repeated every two or three mornings until the fly is exterminated and the plants have grown to go size. When the plants have been set out and are nearly ready to head, the green cabbage worm makes it appearance, and if fine marketable heads are desired this pest must be destroyed. Many remedies for this are given, most of which are ineffectual. It is best to sprinkle well with tar water, taking care to get it well down into the centre of the loose leaves, using an ordinary watering pot for the purpose; if a garden syringe is at hand, it can be thrown into the plant much better than by sprinkling. To make the tar water, the tar is put in a barrel of water and well stirred; then, when it has been allowed to settle, the water from the top is dipped off and used. It should be strong enough to have quite a decided taste.

From HOW AND WHAT TO GROW IN A KITCHEN GARDEN OF ONE ACRE

To Get Rid of Grubs.——The carrot crop is rendered useless in many gardens by grubs eating into the roots. This takes place in many well-managed gardens. The best remedy is to scatter a quantity of soot and lime over the surface of the ground before forking it over for the carrots. This works it into the ground, and keeps the soil free from all sorts of grubs for the whole season. The next best way is to sow the lime and soot between the rows and hoe it into the ground.

Sulphur and Tobacco.——A mixture of sulphur and finely ground tobacco, two parts of the former to one of the latter, has been found an excellent preventive of the ravages of insects on squash and other vines.

To Destroy Bugs on Vines.——To destroy bugs on squash and cucumber vines, dissolve a tablespoonful of saltpetre in a pailful of water; put one pint of this around each hill, shaping the earth so that it will not spread much, and the thing is done. Use more saltpetre if you can afford it——it is good for vegetable, but death to animal life. The bugs burrow in the earth at night and fail to rise in the morning.

From THE NATIONAL FARMER'S AND HOUSE-KEEPER'S CYCLOPAEDIA, 1888

Some Simple Solutions

• • • • •

It is necessary that the gardener should have a hogshead set in the ground always at hand in dry weather, containing solutions made of waste tobacco, lime, soot, elder, burdock leaves, etc. A portion of these ingredients, or any other preparation that is pernicious or poisonous to insects, without injuring the plants, thrown into a hogshead kept filled up with water, if used moderately over beds of young plants in dry weather, would, in almost every case, insure a successful crop. Such liquid, however, should never be used when the sun shines; and if applied too abundantly to the leaves, there is danger, sometimes, that the leaves and stems will be destroyed.

Saltpetre is pernicious to many species of insects; it is also an excellent manure, and may be used to great advantage when dissolved in the proportion of one pound to four gallons of water. This liquid, applied to plants through the rose of a watering-pot, will preserve health and vigor. Soapsuds are equally beneficial, if used occasionally in the same manner—say once a week. These remedies, applied alternately, have been known to preserve melon and cucumber-vines from the ravages of the yellow-fly, bugs, blight, etc., and to keep the plants in a thriving condition.

From the 1866 book, THE AMERICAN GARDENER'S ASSISTANT

◆ ◆ ◆ ◆ ◆

Mealy bugs can be destroyed by syringing with soap suds and kerosene. Make the suds of home-made soap, rather strong, and add a teaspoonful of oil to a gallon of suds, mixing thoroughly before applying. Apply with a good brass syringe that will throw the material forcibly against the foliage. Use once a week, and syringe with clean water daily. This treatment will soon entirely destroy the mealy bug, one of the most tenacious of our insect pests.

From PARKS FLORAL MAGAZINE, 1893

◆ ◆ ◆ ◆ ◆

A decoction of the Tomato plant proves a valuable insecticide. The stems and leaves are boiled in water, which, when cold, is used upon plants affected with insects; it is applied with a syringe, or plant-sprinkler. It destroys green-fly, caterpillars, &c., and leaves upon the plant an odor which prevents the attack of insects for a long time. The remedy is stated to be more effectual than fumigating and washing.

From VICKS MONTHLY MAGAZINE, 1879

◆ ◆ ◆ ◆ ◆

For the last five years I have not lost a cucumber or a melon vine or a cabbage plant. Get a barrel with a few gallons of tar in it; pour water on the tar; always have it ready when needed, and, when the bugs appear, give them a liberal drink of the tar water from a garden sprinkler or otherwise, and, if the rain washes it off and they return, repeat the dose. It will also destroy the Colorado potato beetle, and frighten the old long potato bug worse than a threshing with a brush. Five years ago this summer both kinds appeared on my late potatoes, and I watered with the tar water. The next day all Colorados that had not been protected from the sprinkler were dead, and the others, their name was legion, were all gone, and I have never seen one on the farm since. I am aware that many will look upon this with indifference, because it is so simple and cheap a remedy. Such should always feed their own and their neighbors' bugs, as they frequently do.

Potato Juice as an Insect Destroyer.——As an insect destroyer the juice of the potato plant is said to be of great value; the leaves and stems are well boiled in water, and when the liquid is cold it is sprinkled over plants attacked with insects, when it at once destroys caterpillars, black and green flies, gnats, and other enemies to vegetables, and in no way impairs the growth of the plants. A peculiar odor remains, and prevents insects from coming again for a long time.

From THE NATIONAL FARMER'S AND HOUSE-KEEPER'S CYCLOPAEDIA, 1888

Good Uses for Tobacco

"I find, " says a writer in the NEW ENGLAND HOMESTEAD, "that cabbage needs more hoeing and stirring of the soil than almost any other crop. Neither do I approve of too much stable manure, except for an early crop, for it has a tendency to dry the soil and does not furnish potash enough. I had much rather have tobacco stems or stalks, cut up fine and plowed under broadcast."

◆ ◆ ◆ ◆ ◆

It may be necessary, if insects are numerous, to sow tobacco-dust, mixed with road-dust, soot ashes, lime, or the dust of charcoal, in the proportion of half a bushel per acre every morning, until the plants are free or secure from their attacks.

From the 1866 book, THE AMERICAN GARDENER'S ASSISTANT

How to Grow Tobacco

• • • • •

To raise tobacco, select a sheltered situation, where the young plants can receive the full force of the sun; burn over the surface of the ground early in spring (new land is best), rake it well, and sow the seeds; have a dry, mellow, rich soil, and after a shower, when the plants have got leaves the size of a quarter-dollar, transplant as you would cabbage plants, three and one-half feet apart, and weed out carefully afterward. Break off the suckers from the foot-stalks, as they appear; also the tops of the plants when they are well advanced, say about three feet high, except those designed for seed, which should be the largest and best plants. The ripeness of tobacco is known by small dusky spots appearing on the leaves. The plants should then be cut near the roots, on the morning of a day of sunshine, and should lie singly to wither. When sufficiently withered, gather them carefully together, and hang them up under cover to cure and prepare for market.

From THE NATIONAL FARMER'S AND HOUSE-KEEPER'S CYCLOPAEDIA, 1888

Starting Asparagus

Plow out furrows in well-prepared soil, at least five feet apart, and 10 or 12 inches deep, or if less, at least as deep as depth of surface soil will allow. Then scatter a few inches of rich, well-rotted compost into the furrows, fill in about as much soil, mixing this well with the manure, and set the plants, good, strong, one-year-old to be preferred, at least two feet apart, each upon a little mound of soil and with roots nicely and evenly spread, in the manner shown in picture, and at such a depth that the crowns will be about 7 inches below the ground level. Then cover with two inches of soil, and another dressing of fine rich compost. As the plants grow, and in the due process of cultivation by horse, the furrows are gradually filled up level with the surface. The bed should be kept well cultivated, and free from weeds. The first season some hoed crop, like potatoes, cabbages, radishes, turnips, etc., might be grown between the rows, but in that case the application of the fertilizer required to make up for the removed plant food must not be neglected. In the fall, and every fall afterwards, the tops are to be cut before they shed their seed, taken off the field, or piled up and burned. The young plants, that spring up from seed carelessly left to drop, are sometimes worse than weeds. Winter protection by covering with coarse litter or otherwise is not needed except at the extreme north. The stalks should all be left to grow the next (second) season, and the same thorough cultivation and general treatment given as in the first. In the spring apply a top dressing of good compost.

By T. Greiner, from his 1894 book, HOW TO MAKE THE GARDEN PAY

Hints on Growing Parsley

No garden is complete without a parsley bed, and nothing looks prettier or more ornamental. It is not only useful in soups, but for garnishing dishes of meats and vegetables it cannot be surpassed. The only objection to it is its slow germination. As a small bed of parsley is sufficient for a family garden, the labor necessary to its cultivation is trifling, as the attention to a few square yards of ground can hardly be considered an encroachment upon regular work. It is a native of Sardinia and loves warm weather, but owing to the length of time required for the seeds to germinate, it should be sown very early. If the seed is soaked for twenty-four hours in warm water, previous to sowing, they will sprout in shorter time, or, what is better, mix them with earth dampened with warm water, and keep near the stove in a box until the seeds burst. The earth in the box should not be allowed to become dry from evaporation, but the moisture should be kept by frequent additions of warm water, care being observed not to have it too wet. The ground should be very rich, with well-rotted manure if any is used, spaded deep and fine, and well raked, in order that not the smallest lump or stone may remain. Then sow the seed in rows, mixed with radish, and cover lightly. As the radish will soon push through and show the rows, the weeds can be kept down with the hand.

From THE NATIONAL FARMER'S AND HOUSE-KEEPER'S CYCLOPAEDIA, 1888

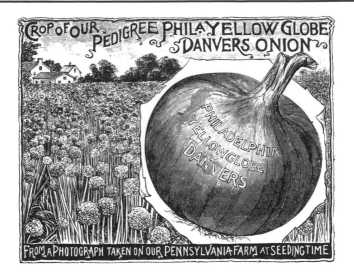

CROP OF OUR PEDIGREE PHILA YELLOW GLOBE DANVERS ONION

PHILADELPHIA YELLOW GLOBE DANVERS

FROM A PHOTOGRAPH TAKEN ON OUR PENNSYLVANIA FARM AT SEEDING TIME

How to Grow Onions

Onion Growing.——A successful gardener writes: Let me say to those who, by reason of repeated failures, have become discouraged, and abandoned the growing of onions, that if they will put the following directions in practice they will be astonished at the result. One of the most important and first considerations is the soil, for it is of no more use to try on unsuitable soil that it is to "spit against the wind," and if you attempt it you will only "get your labor for your pains." The soil must be clean, rich, and light, not a gravelly kind, or one so dry as to suffer from drouth——sandy loam is the best. The sowing should be done in April, and as early in the month as possible; "delay is dangerous." With a heavy roller, or the feet, or in some way, the ground in which the seeds lie should be pressed down quite hard. Weeding should be attended to as soon as you can safely do so. The tops should be left on the bed or field to rot, or to spade or plow in; and onions improve by being grown on the same ground year after year.

A New Method of Raising Onions.——A new method of

onion-growing is strongly recommended by a French horticulturist. Some of the seedlings in the original bed should be left standing at intervals of about a couple of inches, and the spaces between them caused by the removal of the rest, filled in with good garden mold mixed with guano.

The beds must be kept well watered, and it is said the resulting crop will astonish the grower.

Bending Down Onions.——Many old truck farmers have caused surprise to lookers-on at their work, to see them bending over their onion tops. The time to do this is when some begin to show signs of flowering. The method is thus explained: "This operation may be done by the hand, but time is saved by two persons each holding one of the ends of a pole in such a manner as to strike the stems an inch or two above the bulbs. This is called 'laying over,' and is of great benefit to all crops of onions, as the growth of the stems is thereby much checked, and the whole nourishment thrown into the bulbs. It is an old practice in family gardens, and has never failed to give satisfactory results."

From THE NATIONAL FARMER'S AND HOUSE-KEEPER'S CYCLOPAEDIA, 1888

A Trellis for Beans

I prefer to grow the Limas and other running sorts on a
trellis instead of poles. The illustration shows a small
section of what I am tempted to call a model trellis for this
purpose. Heavy posts are set firmly and deeply into the
ground at the ends of each row, and smaller or stout stakes
at intervals of 18 or 20 feet between them. The upper end
of posts and stakes is sawed off square at a height of five
feet, and in line, so that a perfectly straight wire can be
run from end to end over the tops, where it is held by
simple wire staples, but firmly fastened to the end posts,
which, for safety's sake, should be firmly braced. A lighter
wire or twine is run from post to post at a height of about
6 inches from the ground, and common white cotton yarn
wound zig-zag around the two wires (or the wire and
twine). Usually I have a row of Limas, etc., in this shape
on one side of my kitchen garden, running its entire
length, and fully four feet away from other vegetables, in
order to give a fair chance for thorough horse work. I also
aim to set the posts straight and uniform, to stretch the
wires reasonably tight, and to adjust the yarn regularly;
and I can assure you that this trellis is not only useful, but
when vine-clad, also quite an ornament to the garden. With
such a trellis the vines require very little attention in the
way of fastening to the strings. The latter are so
temptingly near, that the runners take hold without much
coaxing.

One of the most important advantages of this trellis

style over the pole method, I find is the opportunity which it affords us to plant the Limas in a continuous row. Here I use plenty of seed, for I am anxious to secure a full stand, and prefer pulling up plants rather than have vacant spots that spoil the looks of the whole, and materially diminish the yield. Should a bare space occur after all, it is easy enough to fill it with plants taken up from where they stand pretty thickly. Lima beans transplant quite readily, especially if lifted after a rain. Carefully take up a clump of soil with a few plants on it, on spade or trowel, and set where needed to fill a gap.

From the 1984 book, HOW TO MAKE THE GARDEN PAY

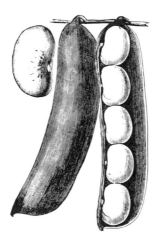

Experiments to Try

A practical gardener makes the following statement: "Last year, as a test of a frequent practice among growers of melons and squashes, I pinched the ends of the long main shoots of the melons, squashes, and cucumbers, and left some to run at their own will. One squash-plant sent out a single stem reaching more than forty feet, but did not bear any fruit. Another plant was pinched until it formed a compact mass of intermingling side-shoots eight feet square, and it bore sixteen squashes. The present year a muskmelon-plant thus pinched in, covered the space allotted to it, and it set twenty-three specimens of fruit; the most of them were pinched off. The pinching causes many lateral branches, which latter produce the female or fertile blossoms, while the main vines produce only the male blossoms. The difference in favor of the yield of an acre of melons treated by this pinching process may easily amount to 100 barrels."

Radishes may be grown in a few days by the following method: Let some good radish seed soak in water for twenty-four hours, and then put them in a bag and expose to the sun. In the course of the day germination will commence. The seed must then be sown in a well-manured hot-bed, and watered from time to time in lukewarm water. By this treatment the radishes will, in a very short time, acquire quite a large bulk, and be very good to eat.

From THE NATIONAL FARMER'S AND HOUSE-KEEPER'S CYCLOPAEDIA, 1888

Tomato Hints

It frequently happens, when the season is late, that the plants have grown a foot, or even two feet, in height or length. This is no disadvantage, but rather a help, if treated in the following manner: A gutter two or three inches in depth and nearly the length of the plant, is scraped under the planting line with the hoe, and the plants laid lengthwise in this and covered over, all but about five or six inches of the top, which is bent straight upward and afterward treated as though it were a plant of that size; the long stem under-ground immediately forms roots and assists in feeding the growth of the plant.

Constant picking as fast as they ripen, and not allowing surplus ones to remain on the vines, will greatly prolong the bearing period.

If the full-sized, green and partly ripe tomatoes are picked off when there is danger of frost, and placed under the sash of the cold frame, or on the floor of the cellar, they will ripen gradually, and though not of very fine quality, may be had fresh almost until Christmas; they must, of course, be entirely green when picked, to consume so much time in ripening.

If some plants of the golden or yellow varieties are planted, they will add greatly to the attractiveness of the dish when mingled with the red ones, served sliced in the ordinary manner.

From the 1888 book, HOW AND WHAT TO GROW IN A KITCHEN GARDEN OF ONE ACRE

Hints on Melons & Cucumbers

Boxes for Melons and Cucumbers.——It is a good plan to make boxes, say twelve inches square and eight inches high, without bottom or top; these, placed over the cucumber or melon hills, and covered with glass, give an impetus to the plants early in the season that nothing short of a hot-bed will effect. If very early, place a little fresh manure around these boxes to keep the contents warm. It is astonishing what an effect this simple contrivance will produce; and not only is it valuable for protection from the cold weather, but it is equally valuable as a protection from melon bugs and other predatory insects that seem to watch for our choicest esculents.

Early Cucumbers and Melons.——For early melons or cucumbers many plant the seeds on inverted sods cut about four inches square. The sods are placed in a frame of any kind, and covered to the depth of half an inch with mellow, rich earth. The plants root firmly in these sods the same as they would in small flower pots, and may safely be transplanted as soon as the weather becomes settled and warm.

Protecting Young Plants.——The striped bug is very destructive to young plants, especially of vines. It is almost impossible to get a stand of early cucumbers, on account of this pest. A writer in one of our exchanges states that a good protection is secured by sheets of cotton wadding. These are placed over the hills before the plants are up, the corners held down with small stones. They are elastic and stretch as the plants grow. The bug cannot get through them. They are also some protection against frost.

A correspondent at Brighton, Ill., writes: "Of course everybody who knows anything at all about melon culture understands that melons do best on warm sandy land, but everybody, perhaps, don't know that I have raised fine melons on heavy clay soil. I put the land in first-rate condition and fertilize in the hill with well-rotted barnyard manure. I also raise the hills a few inches above the level to make the ground warmer and dryer. I never put seed in the ground until the weather is settled and the soil is dry and warm. I use plenty of seed, so as to insure a good stand. The very day the vines begin to show green above ground I begin sprinkling the hills with bone-dust, which operation I repeat every day until they are out of reach of the striped bug, that foe to melon patches. Now I don't say that sprinkling with bone-dust is a sure preventive in all cases to the bug, but it has proved a paying application to me. I have had fewer bugs in my melon patch since I began using it, and it also acts as a tonic to the vines, making them more vigorous. I do not confine the applications of bone dust to melon vines, but use it wherever I fear the striped bugs."

A correspondent of the RURAL NEW YORKER describes the following method by which an extraordinary crop of watermelons was raised: Holes were dug ten feet apart each way, eighteen inches square and fifteen inches deep. These holes were filled with well-rotted manure, which was thoroughly incorporated with the soil. A low, flat hill was then made and seed planted. When the vines were large enough to begin to run, the whole surface was covered to the depth of a foot or fifteen inches with wheat straw. The straw was placed close up around the vines. No cultivation whatever was given afterward; no weeds or grass grew. The vines spread over the straw, and the melons matured clean and nice. The yield was abundant, and the experiment an entire success. This is surely worth trying.

From THE NATIONAL FARMER'S AND HOUSE-KEEPER'S CYCLOPAEDIA, 1888

Companion Planting

◆ ◆ ◆ ◆ ◆

Squash Culture.——A successful raiser of squashes says he manages in this way: I dig holes as deep as I conveniently can with a hoe, six feet apart, close by the side of early peas or potatoes. As soon as the weather will permit I stamp a wheelbarrow of unfermented manure in each hole, pour in a pail of water, and haul over the manure six inches of earth, being careful that the hill is no higher than the surrounding surface. Plant ten or twelve seeds in each hill; when they begin to run, thin to two vines in each hill. The potatoes will be fit for family use before the squashes begin to run, and can be dug ahead of them, leaving the ground mellow, so that the squash vines will root at every joint. This is a great saving of ground in a small garden. Train them all one way.

Novel Method of Growing Cabbages.——A novel plan for setting celery and cabbage plants which has several desirable points to recommend it, is to place them between the rows of your potatoes or sweet corn after the last hoeing. The growing corn or potatoes will afford a partial shade which is very desirable at the time of setting the young plants and until they get fully established, and yet ripen and can be removed in time for them to occupy the ground as a second crop. Two crops on one piece of ground with ten dollars' worth of labor and manure will afford more profit than one crop on which five dollars are expended.

Late Tomatoes.——To raise late tomatoes a good plan is to stick into each watermelon hill a tomato plant. They do not interfere with the former, and come in after the garden crop gives out. Those coming in late are the best for canning and putting up for winter use.

From THE NATIONAL FARMER'S AND HOUSE-KEEPER'S CYCLOPAEDIA, 1888

Successful Succession

To get the full benefit of fresh vegetables during the entire season, it is necessary to sow or plant successional crops every two or three weeks, particularly with such crops as Bush Beans, Cabbage, Cauliflower, Sweet Corn, Cress, Cucumber, Lettuce, Peas, Radish, Spinach, and Turnip. Even small areas of ground, if well manured, may double or treble the crop if judiciously sown or planted. For example, the ground first sown in Radishes, Spinach, Turnip, or Lettuce, in April, will have ripened these crops so that the ground can be cleared, dug up, and manured, and again used by the first of June, when such crops as Sweet Corn, Cucumbers, Peas, or Tomatoes can be planted, and so on all through the list, and thus from May to October the table can be daily supplied with fresh vegetables for a moderate sized family, even from a quarter of an acre of ground, if labor is given sufficient to sow one crop after another has been exhausted.

From GARDENING FOR PLEASURE, 1887

Useful Hints

◆ ◆ ◆

Cucumbers on Trellises.——No one who has not tried it can have any idea of the luxurious growth of a cucumber when trained on a stake, which has a set of stubby side branches left along its length, and the crop on some so trained was enormous. By this the vines occupy less space, and it is the natural habit of the cucumber to climb instead of trailing on the ground.

Training Tomatoes.——A housewife, who vouches for the success of her plan, makes these suggestions for tomato training: "When the plants are ready for the garden, make a considerable hill of good compost. Chip manure is excellent, and a quantity of chicken manure is good. After hill is made, drive a long stake through it. This may be six feet high. Set the plant near it. The training will require attention. The plant will immediately begin to sucker, or throw outside shoots, just above each leaf. These must be cut off, and then the plant will run up vigorously. Tie it to the stake, and do not be afraid to use the knife. Keep on cutting each stem that appears in the axil of a leaf, and keep on tying. The first bearing branches come directly from the body of the plant. Remember that the trimming must be continued as long as the plant bears. Thus trained, the fruit is superior in size, quantity, and flavor, besides being less liable to rot or drop off."

Substitute for Bean Poles.——A new England farmer says: "In my own gardening I have found a most satisfactory substitute for bean poles, which latter are not only expensive, but a source of trouble and care. I plant a sunflower seed by each hill of beans, the stock answering the same purpose as the ordinary bean pole, besides providing an excellent feed for my poultry. I have been using for this purpose a mammoth variety of sunflower seed, many of the flowers of which measured fifteen inches across the seed bed."

From THE NATIONAL FARMER'S AND HOUSE-KEEPER'S CYCLOPAEDIA, 1888

Hints on
Your Harvest & Next Year's
Garden

• • •

In 1862, THE AMERICAN AGRICULTURIST illustrated the potential of growing some good-sized pumpkins through seed selection.

♦ ♦ ♦ ♦ ♦

Save Your Seed

It is quite possible to save better seeds than we can buy, and the habit of carefulness in studying the habits of plants secured by growing our own seed will be worth much more to us than the value of the seeds. All our garden plants have been greatly improved from their originals, and none of them probably have reached the limits of their perfection. They can be made to mature earlier, and to produce more abundantly, as those who have made experiments have learned. If the first well-developed seeds of a plant be selected and sown for several years, the offspring will mature earlier, and eventually a new variety will be secured with a fixed early habit. If we select the longest pods of a bean and plant the seed, we shall find the crop true to its parentage, and a more prolific sort will in time be established. It will take time and patience to secure desirable changes, but there is very great satisfaction in seeing our labors result in permanent improvements in our vegetables. It is a little more trouble to save the first mature cabbage, turnip, or beet seed, and to keep it by itself, but it will pay if one can get a variety that will ripen a week earlier. It is particularly important to hasten the maturity of plants of tropical origin, melons, squashes, cucumbers, tomatoes, egg-plants, etc. Select seeds from the earliest perfect specimens and mark the result. Experimental plants should have the advantage of good soil, a southern exposure, and frequent cultivation. A plant with a predisposition to ripen its fruit early would not have a fair chance in a cold clay soil, or upon a northern or western exposure. If we mean to fix the habit of early maturity, all the circumstances must favor the growth of the plant. Aside from the influence which the saving of our own garden seeds will have upon the improvement of fruits and vegetables, the habit in itself is a good one. It is exceedingly convenient in the hurry of the spring gardening to know just where you can find every package of seed you want to plant, securely tied and labeled, with the name and date of gathering. For this purpose let the good housewife make up a few dozen paper bags, and have the packages stored away in the seed box as fast as they are secured.

From THE AMERICAN AGRICULTURIST, 1868

Hints on Saving Seed

In saving seeds only the best specimens of each kind should be saved, and all inferior ones rejected; this is easy enough with such plants as squashes, cucumbers, tomatoes, melons, etc., care being used to save only the earliest, fairest, and most perfect specimens. The seed should be allowed to ripen thoroughly before taking it from the fruit, which will require some weeks with squashes, after gathering from the vine; tomatoes are placed in the sun for a few days, and melon-seeds may be taken directly when the melon is fit to eat; seeds of this nature having a fleshy pulp are usually cleaned by allowing them to ferment in water for a day or two, when the pulp will easily wash off, after which the seed is spread upon a sheet in the sunshine to dry. Seeds of vines keep longer if not allowed to freeze; they will preserve their vitality five or six years if kept in a warm, dry place. A closet near a chimney is a good place, and, since mice and rats are fond of such tidbits as melon-seeds, it will be advisable to lock them up in a tin chest or other rat-proof arrangement. When saving seeds of beets, cabbage, turnip, etc., those who are most particular reject all but the seed grown on the leading stem.

Seeds of all kinds keep best in a dry, even temperature. When to be kept in large lots, they may be put in bags and hung from the ceiling of the room, to keep them from the mice. Most seeds are good from two to five years, if carefully kept; onion-seed, however, is very inferior after the first year, and worthless after the second. When old seed is to be used, it should be previously tested by sowing a counted lot in a hot-bed or other suitable place, and counting the number of plants that come up, and noting the vigor of the plants; the plants from old seed are usually less vigorous than from fresh seed, and sometimes are so weak as to be worthless.

From THE NATIONAL FARMER'S AND HOUSE-KEEPER'S CYCLOPAEDIA, 1888

◆ ◆ ◆ ◆ ◆

It will not do to take off all the best ears of corn, or the tightest heads of lettuce, using the nubbins and runts for seed, or the next year the nubbins will predominate and the lettuce will go to seed without taking the trouble to form a head at all.

The best plan is to set apart a section of the row of each variety for seed, and not gather any for use from that part; here all the nubbins and inferior specimens could be pulled off, throwing the full strength of the plant into the finest fruits; and the same way with the vines; one or more hills, as desired, could be kept for the purpose of bearing seed only.

All seeds should be thoroughly cleaned and dried, and each package should be carefully marked with name and date before storing. The seed chest should be in some cool place where there is no danger of frost or very warm heat, and, most of all, no danger from dampness. It is important to have the date of saving the seed marked, so that when all is not used it may be kept, as frequently a crop fails from a bad season or other causes, and a new lot of equal merit cannot be obtained, the date serving to tell how good the seed is; seed of some vegetables retaining vitality for only two years, and others as long as ten years.

HOW TO SAVE YOUR TOMATO SEEDS

If you save your own seed, the earliest ripened specimens should be saved for that purpose, and should be of perfect shape and evenly ripened, with no core, crack or rot about them. The easiest way to clean this seed is, take a small box, knock the top and bottom off, and nail some wire fly screening over the bottom; take the fresh tomatoes, not rotten ones, as are frequently used, and squeeze the seeds into this sieve, throwing the pulp and flesh away; the seed can be washed free and clean by running clean water upon them, keep them constantly stirred and pick out the bits of pulp as they become free and float upon the top of the water, while the water and finer particles will pass off through the screening. When clean allow all the water to drain off and spread the seeds thinly on a smooth board or cloth in the sun; they should be stirred frequently, to prevent their adhering to each other when dry. If seeds are washed out in this manner and carefully dried, you can depend on every one growing, while from those saved in the ordinary manner, from tomatoes that have been allowed to heat and rot, sometimes not one seed in a hundred will germinate.

From the 1888 book, HOW AND WHAT TO GROW IN A KITCHEN GARDEN OF ONE ACRE

Wintering Root Crops

• • • • •

No difficulty will be experienced in carrying root crops over until spring in pits outdoors, in same way as farmers frequently winter apples and potatoes. Select a dry spot or one for which drainage can easily be provided, and dig an excavation about a foot or 18 inches deep, 6 feet wide, and of the length required to hold the quantity of roots to be wintered over. They are placed on a conical heap, as shown above, covered with six, eight, ten or twelve inches of straw, according to the severity of the winters in the particular locality, and with a foot of soil upon the straw. A whisk of straw or a section of common tile drain, reaching from the straw covering through the soil to the outside, should be adjusted in the centre of every eight or ten foot section to provide the required ventilation. If such a pit is opened before the cold weather has entirely passed, the roots remaining in it need careful covering to guard against freezing.

From the book, HOW TO MAKE THE GARDEN PAY, 1894

Celery Blanching

Earthing-up Celery

Blanching by Boards.

Celery Bleachers.

From the 1894 book, HOW TO MAKE THE GARDEN PAY

Easy Celery Blanching

· · · · ·

The common and laborious process of earthing up and winter storage of celery is doubtless a great obstacle in the way of its culture by many busy farmers. The COUNTRY GENTLEMAN suggests this easy method of blanching, which does away altogether with the necessity of trenches or banking, at least for moderate supplies: "If intended for winter blanching, about the middle of November they are taken up on a dry day and placed in water-tight troughs or other vessels in a quite dark cellar, the plants standing erect and closely together. Enough water is poured on the roots to cover them, and the supply is continued through the winter as it evaporates. This constitutes the entire labor. The stalks are gradually and handsomely blanched in the darkness, and many new ones spring up during the winter months, especially if the apartment is not very cold, and these new shoots are remarkable for their delicacy and perfect freedom from any particle of rust, appearing like polished ivory. A small separate apartment in the cellar, without windows, answers well for this purpose. Boxes, tubs, or any vessels which will hold a few inches of water may be employed. The plants, as grown in the open ground, need not be earthed up at all, or they may be slightly earthed to bring them into a more compact form, if desired. Probably the best way would be to adopt the course which is sometimes employed of setting out the plants in summer on the level surface of deep, rich soil, eight or ten inches or a foot apart each way, in order that their close growth may tend to give them a more upright form. They are merely kept clean by hoeing through the season."

From THE NATIONAL FARMER'S AND HOUSE-KEEPER'S CYCLOPAEDIA, 1888

Wintering Cabbages

Methods of Wintering.—There are numerous ways in which cabbages can be kept successfully for home use, or the often good market during latter part of winter or early spring. A general rule is applicable to all methods. It is this, to pull the crop on a dry day, and pack it only when perfectly dry. Also put off the final covering, or storing in buildings, cellars, etc., as long in the fall as can be safely done. One of the most commonly practised methods is to wrap the outer leaves of each plant firmly around the head, and stand root side up closely together, either in single line or in a close double row, with or without another layer on top; then plow a furrow from each side to the ridge of cabbages thus formed, and finish covering up with soil, using shovel or spade, leaving only the extremities of the roots sticking out. The illustration represents a cross section of each of the three arrangements. Another good way to store cabbages is to put them in pits, like root crops. The excavation is made 6 or 8 inches deep, 4 feet wide, and as long as needed to make room for the quantity of cabbages desired to store. Here the heads are packed in a conical heap, roots inward, and covered with 8 or 10 inches of soil, packed firmly. In case we should want to use all or part of them during the winter, it will be a good precaution to cover the south side of pit with straw or other dry litter deep enough to keep the soil from freezing, and thus secure easy access to the cabbages whenever wanted.

From the book, HOW TO MAKE THE GARDEN PAY, 1894

Preparations for Next Year's Garden

The gases arising from the decaying of the coarse manure in the soil tend to lighten it, instead of being wasted in the air, as is the case when the manure is in heaps or in the barnyard. By plowing-time in the spring the manure will have assimilated with the soil and will be thoroughly worked through the cultivated surface, thus affording food for the crops in all stages. If such manure is applied in the spring, it will make dry or thin soil still drier, and unless plowed well under, where it would take the roots a long time to reach it, will burn the young plants up if the season should happen to be a dry one. The great value of compost in starting young plants is that it affords rich food in proper form for the tender young rootlets, enabling the young plants to make a quick, tender growth, which is very essential if vegetables of fine quality are desired. By fall manuring and plowing the whole garden is composted, while the action of the frost on the lumps and ridges pulverizes them, leaving the soil in a fine, friable condition.

From the 1888 book, HOW AND WHAT TO GROW IN A KITCHEN GARDEN OF ONE ACRE

♦ ♦ ♦ ♦ ♦

There are very few people not fond of Lettuce in the early spring. Having removed from the city, where early Lettuce could be bought at the markets, I was much at a loss for this refreshing salad plant—at least, until quite warm weather. Knowing it to be quite hardy, I last autumn sowed some seed in a warm, dry spot, and in a week or two the plants were up. Before hard frost, I placed around my little patch some boards—to be particular, an old door frame—and over this some loose boards, covering about two-thirds of the space, so that there was about one-third uncovered for light and air. It was where it got the best of the sun, sloping southeast, and it was a surprise to find how early I had young Lettuce from this rude bed. Of course, this will be of no benefit to those who have hot-beds and other conveniences for forcing vegetables.

To get early Pie Plant, just place an old barrel over the root in the fall, and throw around the barrel a lot of manure, or old straw and refuse, and in spring the Pie Plant will start and produce leaves wonderfully early. Some think putting the barrel over in the spring is just as good, but I am convinced the autumn is the best time.

From VICK'S MONTHLY MAGAZINE, 1880

♦ ♦ ♦ ♦ ♦

In winter, while there is plenty of time before the spring opens, the summer campaign should be planned—what vegetables are to be raised and what quantity of each will be needed, in what part of the garden it will be best to plant each variety so that the pollen from different members of the same family, such as cucumbers and cantaloupes, will not mix and spoil each other's fine flavor. If the soil is of different quality in different parts of the garden, it should be planned so that the heavy and the lighter portions shall be occupied by such crops as will succeed best in the respective soils.

Ease of cultivation and the rotation or succession of crops should also be considered. The small-growing plants which require hand hoeing should be together, and likewise those which are to be worked with the horse cultivator. Where the ground is to bear two crops——one planted after the other has matured and been taken off——it will be of advantage to have such crops together, thus making larger plots for the replowing and a consequent saving of time and work.

From the 1888 book, HOW AND WHAT TO GROW IN A KITCHEN GARDEN OF ONE ACRE

WEED THIS FALL

What, now, when the growing season is so nearly over? Yes, now, emphatically NOW. Just at this season, especially in the potato fields and gardens, and by the sides of fences everywhere, weeds are ripening their seeds and scattering them far and wide over the surrounding land. Special care is needful, therefore, to subdue these interlopers. Go through the fields, at once, and cut down or pull up the luxuriant weeds before they ripen their seeds and scatter them in myriads over the field. By all means pull up those in the garden. Pile them all in heaps, and as soon as partially dry, mix them in a brush heap and burn them, or better, add them to the manure heap, where fermentation destroys the vitality of the seeds.

From the November, 1962 issue of THE AMERICAN AGRICULTURIST

Rotate Next Year's Garden

• • • • •

When it comes to the second or succeeding seasons, the crop or crops raised in the plot the year before must be taken into account. The situation of the crop of each particular vegetable should be moved to another part, as each draws certain proportions of the food elements from the soil, and those of a different character should occupy the ground in rotation, that the soil may be kept in the richest state. Thus the quality or size of the crop will not be lessened by being planted in a situation that it has depleted, to some extent, of its own particular food the year before. Reference should also be had to the kind of food which the plant requires, as in the case of strawberries and potatoes, which should not succeed each other without special manures, as they both exhaust, to a great extent, the potash in the soil, so that the soil, having borne a heavy crop of one, would of necessity make but a poor return of the other if planted in direct succession. If this cannot be overcome by a change of location, the gardener will know that the proper food elements have been depleted by the previous crop, and must try to supply them with special manure or commercial fertilizers.

From The 1888 book, HOW AND WHAT TO GROW IN A KITCHEN GARDEN OF ONE ACRE

Hints on Crop Rotation

It is proved by experience, that fall Spinach is an excellent preparative for Beets, Carrots, Radishes, Salsify, and all other tap, as well as tuberous-rooted vegetables.

Celery or Potatoes constitute a suitable preparative for Cabbage, Cauliflower, and all other plants of the Brassica tribe; as also Artichokes, Asparagus, Lettuce, and Onions, provided such ground be well situated, which is a circumstance always to be duly considered in laying out a garden.

Lands that have long laid in pasture are, for the first three or four years after being tilled, superior for Cabbage, Turnips, Potatoes, etc., and afterwards for culinary vegetables in general.

The following rules are subjoined for further government:

Fibrous-rooted plants may be alternated with tap or tuberous-rooted, and vice versa.

Plants which produce luxuriant tops, so as to shade the land, should be succeeded by such as yield small tops or narrow leaves.

Those which, during their growth, require the operation of stirring the earth, should precede such as do not require cultivation.

Ground which has been occupied by Artichokes, Asparagus, Rhubarb, Sea Kale, or such other crops as remain long on a given spot, should be subjected to a regular rotation of crops for at least as long a period as it remained under such permanent crops. Hence in all gardens judiciously managed, the Strawberry-bed is changed every three or four years, till it has gone the circuit of all the compartments; and Asparagus-beds should be renewed, on the same principle, as often as they fail to produce luxuriantly. Indeed, no two crops should be allowed to ripen their seed in succession in the same soil, if it can be avoided.

By Thomas Bridgeman, from his 1866 book, THE AMERICAN GARDENER'S ASSISTANT

Save Your Leaves

Leaves are the natural mulch. Go into the woods in autumn and look under the leaves and you will find various seeds sprouting under them and getting a sufficient start to enable them to winter under this genial covering, and break into vigorous growth with the return of spring. The beautiful wild flowers, which die out when taken to the garden, are in the woods nicely tucked up under a coverlet of leaves; they sleep warm and awake strong and refreshed. There is no better winter covering for a strawberry bed, and for herbaceous plants generally, than a good coating of leaves. The great difficulty is, they will blow away. This may be prevented by laying brush upon them, or giving them a light sprinkling of soil. Plants protected in this way have a covering which will ward off the injurious effects of sudden changes of temperature, but will not pack so closely as to endanger the health of the plant. Decomposed leaves are valuable, and in the form of leaf mould are considered one of the chief fertilizers. Aside from the purely vegetable matter they contain, the leaves have also a great deal of mineral matter which is deposited in them during the constant evaporation that is carried on during the growing season. This mineral matter is in just that finely divided and soluble state which makes it ready to be again taken up by other plants. The leaves of trees when burned, give from ten to thirty per cent more ashes than the wood of the same tree. It will be seen that leaves are of the highest value in the compost heap. He who neglects to save them disregards the sources of fertility which nature is kindly offering him. Early in autumn many leaves will fall, and the collection should be begun and continued, and any place, large or small, will find a well sheltered pile of leaves valuable to draw upon for mulch, for winter covering, and for use in equal proportion with manure in hot-beds. Those not needed for these purposes may add to the richness of the manure heap. By all means save the leaves.

From an 1864 issue of THE AMERICAN AGRICULTURIST

Useful Rules, Tables & Hints

* * * * *

How Long Will Seeds Keep?

There is no general answer to the question, as seeds of different kinds, collected and preserved with equal care, will vary in the length of time they retain their powers of germination. Some seem to be good after an indefinite period, while others are not to be depended upon after they are a year old. The seeds of some trees will not germinate at all if once allowed to dry, and others will only appear the second year after planting. Works upon horticulture are generally deficient in information upon the raising of seeds and the length of time they may be safely kept. While it is safest to keep them at a uniform temperature just above freezing, there are many which will bear great extremes of heat and cold. Plants have been raised from seeds taken from raspberry jam which must have been exposed to a heat of 220 degrees. When buried in the earth, below the reach of those influences which induce germination, there seems to be no limit to the vitality of some seeds.——Among plants commonly cultivated, the seeds of carrots, onions, parsneps, and salsafy, are not to be relied upon when over a year old. Beets, spinach, lettuce, celery and parsley, will keep 2 or 3 years. Radishes, cabbages and turnips, 4 or 5 years. Melons and cucumbers may be kept for 10 or more years; old seeds of these are preferred by some gardeners, as the vines are said to be more prolific and less luxuriant than those from fresh ones. Good seeds being heavier than water will generally sink in it, but this is not applicable to those with a hairy or spongy seed-coat; such seeds will float even when Sound. The only sure test is to try to sprout them in boxes or pots or earth. If they do not germinate there, they should be rejected.

From THE AMERICAN AGRICULTURIST, 1863

Rules for Gardeners

1. Perform every operation in the proper season and in the best manner.
2. Complete every operation consecutively.
3. Never, if possible, perform one operation in such a manner as to render another necessary.
4. When called off from any operation, leave your work and tools in an orderly manner.
5. In leaving off work, make a temporary finish, and clean your tools and carry them to the tool-house.
6. Never do that in the garden or hothouses, which can be equally well done in the reserve ground or in the back sheds.
7. Never pass a weed or an insect without pulling it up or taking it off, unless time forbid.
8. In gathering a crop, take away the useless as well as the useful parts.
9. Let no plant ripen seeds, unless they are wanted for some purpose, useful or ornamental, and remove all parts which are in a state of decay.

By J. C. Louden, as published in the 1892 book, THE HORTICULTURISTS' RULE BOOK

THE BEST TIME FOR SOWING OR SETTING PLANTS
MICHIGAN

```
Bean, Bush . . . . . . . . . . . . . . . . . . . . May 16
  ", Pole . . . . . . . . . . . . . . . . . . . . May 30
Beet . . . . . . . . . . . . . . . . . . . . . . April 20
Broccoli . . . . . . . . . . . . . . . . . . . . May 10
Brussels Sprouts . . . . . . . . . . . . . . . . May 10
Cabbage, early, under glass . . . . . . . . . . March 15
Cabbage, late . . . . . . . . . . . . . . . . . May 20
Carrot . . . . . . . . . . . . . . . . . . . . . May 7
Cauliflower, under glass . . . . . . . . . . . . March 15
Celery, under glass . . . . . . . . . . . . . . March 18
  ", in open ground . . . . . . . . . . . . . . May 20
Corn . . . . . . . . . . . . . . . . . . . . . . May 19
Cucumber . . . . . . . . . . . . . . . . . . . . May 23
Egg-Plant, under glass . . . . . . . . . . . . . March 15
Kale . . . . . . . . . . . . . . . . . . . . . . May 9
Kohlrabi . . . . . . . . . . . . . . . . . . . . May 9
Lettuce . . . . . . . . . . . . . . . . . . . . . May 5
Melon . . . . . . . . . . . . . . . . . . . . . May 30
Okra . . . . . . . . . . . . . . . . . . . . . . May 15
Onion . . . . . . . . . . . . . . . . . . . . . April 17
Parsnips . . . . . . . . . . . . . . . . . . . . May 7
Pepper, under glass . . . . . . . . . . . . . . March 16
Peas . . . . . . . . . . . . . . . . . . . . . . April 15
Potato . . . . . . . . . . . . . . . . . . . . . May 3
Pumpkin . . . . . . . . . . . . . . . . . . . . May 31
Radish . . . . . . . . . . . . . . . . . . . . . April 26
Salsify . . . . . . . . . . . . . . . . . . . . . May 7
Spinage . . . . . . . . . . . . . . . . . . . . April 10
Squash . . . . . . . . . . . . . . . . . . . . . May 28
Tomato, under glass . . . . . . . . . . . . . . March 13
Turnip . . . . . . . . . . . . . . . . . . . . . April 15
```

From THE HORTICULTURISTS' RULE BOOK, 1892

THE BEST TIME FOR SOWING OR SETTING PLANTS
MASSACHUSETTS

Asparagus . . . . .About the end of April.

Bean, Bush . . . . . . .About the first week in May.

Bean, Pole . . . . . . .From about the middle of May
to the 1st of June.

Bean, Lima . . . . . . .About the 1st of June.

Beet . . . . .About the middle of April.

Borecole, or Kale . . . .About the middle of April; plant
out in June.

Brussels Sprouts . . . . .In March or April in hotbed.

Cabbage . . . . .Transplant the last week in April
or the 1st in May.

Carrots . . . . .Last of May or 1st of June.

Cauliflower . . . . . . .From the 1st of May until the
1st of July.

Celery . . . . .The 1st week in April to the 2nd
in July.

Corn, Sweet . . . . . .About the 1st of May.

Cucumber . . . . .For 1st crop, about the middle
of March.

Egg-Plant . . . . .About March 15th in hotbed.

Endive . . . . .June or July.

Kohlrabi . . . . .May or June.

Okra . . . . .About the 10th of May.

Peas . . . . .During the last of April up to the
1st of May.

Pepper . . . . .Put out of doors about the 1st of
April.

Radish . . . . .From the 1st of April to the
Middle of June.

Spinage . . . . .About the 1st of September.

Tomato . . . . .About the 25th of May set plants
outdoors.

Turnips, for all use . . . .Any time from July 1st to
August 20th.

Watermelon . . . . . . .About the middle of May.

From THE HORTICULTURISTS' RULE BOOK, 1892

THE BEST TIME FOR SOWING OR SETTING PLANTS

GEORGIA

Asparagus . . . . . .From December 1st to the middle of March.

Bean, Bush . . . . .From the 1st to the middle of March.

Beet . . . . .Through November and December.

Cabbage . . . . . .From the 1st of October to the 15th. Transplant about November 1st and later.

Cauliflower . . . . .From May to September.

Cucumber . . . . . .About March 1st to the 15th.

Egg-Plant . . . . . .To prick out, about the middle of January, otherwise ten or fifteen days later.

Lettuce . . . . . . .About the middle of September.

Onion . . . . . . .About January 1st.

Pea . . . . .About December 1st.

Potato . . . . . . .The 1st of February.

Radish . . . . . . .From Christmas to the last of February.

Spinage . . . . . .From September 10th until October 15th.

Squash . . . . . .About the last of February up to the middle of March.

Sweet-Potato . . . .In coldframes, about the 1st of January.

Tomato . . . . . .About January 1st.

Watermelon . . . .About the 15th of March.

From THE HORTICULTURISTS' RULE BOOK, 1892

THE BEST DISTANCES FOR PLANTING

Artichoke . . . . . .Rows 3 or 4 ft. apart, 2 to 3 ft. apart in the row.

Asparagus . . . . . .Rows 3 to 4 ft. apart, 1 to 2 ft. apart in the row.

Beans, Bush . . . . .1 ft. apart in rows 2 to 3 ft. apart.

Bean, Pole . . . . .3 to 4 ft. each way.

Beet, early . . . . .In drills 12 to 18 in. apart.

 " late . . . . . .In drills 2 to 3 ft. apart.

Broccoli . . . . . .1½ x 2½ ft. to 2 x 3 ft;

Cabbage, early . . .16 x 28 in. to 18 x 30 in.

 ", late . . . .2 x 3 ft. to 2½ x 3½ ft.

Carrot . . . . . . .In drills 1 to 2 ft.

Cauliflower . . . . .2 x 2 ft. to 2 x 3 ft.

Celery . . . . . . .Rows 3 to 4 ft. apart, 6 to 9 in. in the row.

Corn-Salad . . . . .In drills 12 to 18 in. apart.

Corn, Sweet . . . .Rows 3 to 3½ ft. apart, 9 in. to 2 ft. in the row.

Cress . . . . .In drills 10 to 12 in. apart.

Cucumber . . . . . .4 to 5 ft. each way.

Egg-Plant . . . . . .3 x 3 ft.

Endive . . . . . . .1 x 1 ft. to 1 x 1½ ft.

Horse-radish . . . .1 x 2 or 3 ft.

Kohlrabi . . . . . .10 x 18 in. to 1 x 2 ft.

Leek . . . . .6 in. x 1 or 1½ ft.

Lettuce . . . . . .1 x 1½ or 2 ft.

From THE HORTICULTURISTS' RULE BOOK, 1892

♦ ♦ ♦

Concerning the distance plants should be apart in the rows or otherwise, it may be safely said that each plant should stand so that when fully matured its outside leaves will just touch those of its nearest neighbor. This rule does not apply to onions and root crops, which may stand closer.

From the 1888 book, HOW AND WHAT TO GROW IN A KITCHEN GARDEN OF ONE ACRE

THE TIME NEEDED FOR PLANTS TO MATURE

Beans, String	. . . . .45-65 days from seed.
Beans, Shell	. . . . .65-70 days from seed.
Beets, Turnip	. . . . .65 days from seed.
Beets, Long Blood	. . . . .150 days from seed.
Cabbage, Early	. . . . .105 days from seed.
Cabbage, Late	. . . . .150 days from seed.
Cauliflower	. . . . .110 days from seed.
Corn	. . . . .75 days from seed.
Egg-Plant	. . . . 150-160 days from seed.
Lettuce	. . . . .65 days from seed.
Melon, Water	. . . . 120-140 days from seed.
Melon, Musk	. . . . 120-140 days from seed.
Onion	. . . . 135-150 days from seed.
Pepper	. . . . 140-150 days from seed.
Radish	. . . . .30-45 days from seed.
Squash, Summer	. . . . .60-65 days from seed.
Squash, Winter	. . . . .125 days from seed.
Tomatoes	. . . . .150 days from seed.
Turnips	. . . . .60-70 days from seed.

From THE HORTICULTURISTS' RULE BOOK, 1892

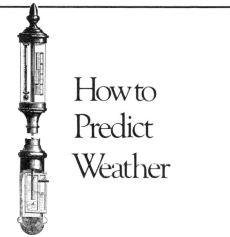

How to Predict Weather

From THE HORTICULTURISTS' RULE BOOK, 1892

Stationary barometer indicates continuance of the present weather.

Slowly rising barometer usually indicates fair weather.

Slowly falling barometer indicates the approach of a severe storm. One-fifth to one-third of an inch is sufficient fall to give indications.

Sudden rise of the barometer indicates the approach of a storm or the breaking-up of an existing storm.

Sudden fall of the barometer indicates high winds and probable rain.

When areas of low and high barometer are near together, heavy gales may be expected.

Long lines of clouds extending up the sky from a common starting-point often fortell a storm from that quarter.

When the fleecy or cirrus clouds settle down into horizontal bars or ribs in the upper sky, wet and foul weather may be expected. This is the "mackerel sky."

If contiguous clouds move in various directions, rain is likely to follow soon.

When small black clouds scud over an overcast sky, heavy rain and bad weather may be expected.

Cumulus clouds that preserve a well-rounded form and float high in the air indicate fair weather.

Anvil-shaped cumulus clouds usually indicate thunder-storms.

In spring and fall, rain is often indicated by a dense bank of gray clouds in the east, in front of which are little shoals of blackish clouds.

Cirro-cumulus clouds—like bunches and fleeces of wool scattered high in the sky—are indications of still and dry weather.

When the rays of the rising sun shoot far up into the sky, fair weather may be expected.

When the ray-like shadows of clouds overlie a hazy sky in the vicinity of the sun, rain is apt to follow. This is expressed in the phrase, "the sun drawing water."

Gaudy hues of blue and purple at sunset prophesy rain and wind.

A bright red sunset means fair weather for the morrow.

A pale and diffuse sun at setting portends a storm.

If the sun sets in subdued purple and the zenith is pale blue, fair weather may be expected.

A deep red morning sky is usually followed by bad weather.

A sonorous condition of the atmosphere foretells rain.

A bank of cloud across the southern horizon in winter indicates snow. It is frequently called the "snow-bank."

If the sun rises clear but becomes overcast within half an hour, prepare for rain.

A halo about the moon indicates a rain-storm.

If the sky is white or yellowish white nearly to the zenith after sunset, prepare for rain soon.

Strong east winds indicate a storm.

Haziness is indicative of dry weather. It is due to dust in the atmosphere.

When haziness suddenly disappears and the sun sets pale and the sky is very clear, rain is probable.

When stars twinkle with unusual prominence, rain may be expected.

Heavy dew indicates fair weather.

Absence of dew for two or three mornings in succession in summer is a precursor of rain.

Shut Your Gate Behind You

When you leave your garden, fruit patch, or grounds, of whatever kind, shut the gate, and leave whatever is behind it, there——don't take it with you. Recollect that when you visit the place of another, you go to see what he has to show, and learn what he has to teach. If you would be a welcome visitor, and be dismissed with a pressing invitation to come again, place yourself in a receptive mood; be for the time the attentive pupil and not the teacher. When others visit your place, will be the proper time to teach. Of all the intolerable bores who visit us is the man who brings his own place with him, and who, whatever may be shown him, at once institutes a comparison with his own, and at once begins to tell that "mine are much better than that,"——"I can beat you on so and so," and ignoring the thing before him tell us, "Ah, you should see my strawberries," "My roses," "My tomatoes," and so on all through——in short, the man who did not "shut his own gate behind him." Those who are so thoroughly satisfied with their own that they can not forget it for a few hours, should not visit, but remain upon the scene of their remarkable achievements——at home. We would not imply that one in visiting the grounds of another, may not, on occasion, drop a useful hint drawn from his own experience, or that he may not give his host any information that he may ask for. But we have been so annoyed at receiving visitors, and worse still, in visiting strange grounds in company with those whose only object in visiting appears to be to boast of their own affairs, that we feel called upon to protest against it.

From THE AMERICAN AGRICULTURIST, 1878

Good Advice

Never delay doing to-day, in the hope of having more time to-morrow. Do it at once, if it can be done. Gardeners have not a moment to spare——unoccupied ground, weeds, hoeing, raking, sowing, reaping, digging——preparing poles, rods, stakes, manure, and many other duties, demand his attention at all times. We have never seen a good gardener who did not feel it a pleasure to be in advance of these wants. Get once behind, lose time, and it is hard to make up. Sow early in the season, and if you fail you have time for a second trial; whereas, if you sow late and miss your crop, the opportunity of recovering the loss is gone with it. Sow before or just after rain, but never when the ground is wet. Beware of sowing deep, or in dry weather, or on dry ground. If this cannot be avoided, soak your seeds in water a few hours, sow them, and then water the ground freely. Gardeners never sleep when the sun is up.

From BRUIST'S FAMILY KITCHEN GARDEN, 1847

For convenience in sowing by hand it is always advisable to moisten the fertilizer before it is applied. Empty a bagful on a tight barn floor, or in a tight wagon box, spread the fertilizer out in an even layer, then sprinkle water over it; next put on another layer of fertilizer, apply water as before, and finally shovel the whole mass over until it is thoroughly mixed, and uniformly damp. It can then be sowed without filling the air around the party whose hands scatter it, with the disagreeable dust.

From the book, HOW TO MAKE THE GARDEN PAY, 1894

The best time for watering is in the evening. Though water may be given to the roots at any time, it should never be sprinkled on the foliage in the hot sun, as that causes brown spots or blisters where it comes in contact with the leaves. More injury than good results from beginning to water a plant, and then not keeping it up till the necessity ceases. As soon as the ground begins to get dry after watering, the soil should be stirred with the hoe. When you start to water a plant, do it thoroughly, so as to give the roots a soaking at every watering, or else do not water at all.

From The 1888 book, HOW AND WHAT TO GROW IN A KITCHEN GARDEN OF ONE ACRE

The main points to be regarded in transplanting, are handling the plant carefully, so as to injure the roots as little as possible, planting firmly and shading to prevent the sun from withering or scorching the leaves. It should be borne in mind, that it is not nature's design that a plant should be transplanted, and we ought to show sympathy.

From the 1888 book, HOW AND WHAT TO GROW IN A KITCHEN GARDEN OF ONE ACRE

And now, having taken a walk with you through the kitchen garden, all I have further to say is, may you be favored with seasonable rain and sunshine, for, be it remembered, without the co-operation of the elements all our efforts are in vain.

From the 1888 book, HOW AND WHAT TO GROW IN A KITCHEN GARDEN OF ONE ACRE

SEED SOURCES

• • • • •

According to the National Gardening Association, there are over 700 seed catalogs. The variety of vegetables that you can grow in your "kitchen garden" is endless.

This brief list of seed catalogs presents sources for hard-to-find traditional vegetables, heirloom varieties and open-pollinated, non-hybrid vegetables. Match the key number or letter of the type of vegetable that you're looking for with those listed with each seed company. Catalogs are free unless a price is noted.

HARD-TO-FIND TRADITIONAL VEGETABLES — Cardoon (1), Chervil (2), Chicory (3), Corn Salad (4), Cress (5), Dandelion (6), Fennel (7), Jerusalem Artichoke (8), Martynia (9), New Zealand Spinach (10), Nasturtium (11), Okra (12), Pop Corn (13), Salsify (14), Scorzonera (15), Sea Kale (16), Shallots (17), Skirret (18), Sorrel (19), Upland Cress (20), Vegetable Marrow (21), Water Cress (22).

HEIRLOOM VEGETABLES (H) — Many old varieties of vegetables have been preserved by home gardeners and hobbyists and by horticulturists at living history museums across the country. These varieties were developed, in the past, for individual advantages, such as: better winter storage; great taste; better adaptability to a certain climate; earlier yield; brighter color for a more decorative garden; drought resistance — the advantages and the varieties are endless. Like the advice in this book, heirloom seeds are a legacy from yesterday's gardeners.

OPEN-POLLINATED VEGETABLES (P) — The seeds of modern hybrid vegetables can't be saved. They'll either not grow or they'll produce a plant that is very different from, and usually inferior to, its parent. If you want to save your seed and improve your vegetables from year to year, you'll have to start with open-pollinated varieties.

148

ALLEN, STERLING & LOTHROP, 191 U.S. Route No. 1, Falmouth ME 04105 — 2,5,6,7,10,11,12,13,14, H — full line catalog of vegetables, herbs & flowers.

W. ATLEE BURPEE CO., 300 Park Ave., Warminister, PA 18974 — 3,4,6,7,8,10,13,14,19,20 — founded in 1876, Burpee published the 1888 book, HOW AND WHAT TO GROW IN A KITCHEN GARDEN OF ONE ACRE, quoted in this book. They probably supplied most of this book's 19th Century writers with their seed. — 184p, full color, full line catalog.

BUTTERBROOK FARM, 78 Barry Road, Oxford, CT 06483 (S.A.S.E.) — 10,11,12,13 H, P — this small seed co-op offers a variety of vegetables that thrive in New England's short growing season. All are open-pollinated, for seed-savers and should perform well in most cold regions or for succession planting in the south.

THE COOKS GARDEN, P.O. Box 65, Londonderry, VT 05748 ($1.00) — 2,3,4,5,6,7,10,11,16,19,22 H — 28 varieties of hard-to-find salad greens, 13 chicories, 35 varieties of lettuce.

WILLIAM DAM SEEDS, Box 8400, Dundas, Ontario, L9H 6M1, Canada ($1.00) — 1,2,3,4,5,6,7,8,10,11,12,13,14, 15,19,21,22 — full color, 64p catalog with a great variety of vegetables, herbs, flowers & accessories.

DEGIORGI CO. INC., P.O. Box 413, Council Bluffs, IA 51502 ($1.00) — 1,2,3,4,6,7,9,10,11,12,13,14,19,21,22 — catalog offers vegetables, flowers & decorative plants.

EARL MAY SEED & NURSERY, 208 North Elm Street, Shenandoah, IA 51603 — 1,2,3,10,11,12,13,14, — 79p, full color catalog of vegetables, nursery stock, flowers & accessories.

GOOD SEED CO., P.O. Box 702, Tonasket, WA 98855 ($1.00) — 2,7,11 H, P — informative and easy to read, 64p catalog offers heirloom vegetables and herbs, and a great deal of very good advice on how to grow them. Their

"Pioneer Vegetable Garden" is a collection of 20 varieties popular before 1850.

GRACE'S GARDENS, 10 Bay St., Westport, CT 06880 (25¢) H, P — Jane Grace is famous for setting records with her vegetables. This little catalog offers some very big and unusual vegetables.

GURNEY SEED & NURSERY, 110 Capitol Street, Yankton, SD 57078 — 3,4,7,10,11,12,13,14,15,21,23 — 66p, full line catalog of vegetables & nursery stock.

H.G. HASTINGS CO. — P.O. Box 4274, Atlanta, GA — 10,11,12,13,14 — full color, 64p catalog from the historic (1889) "Seedsman to the South," offers vegetables, herbs, nuts, fruits, tools & books for the home gardener.

HEIRLOOM GARDEN SEEDS, P.O. Box 138, Guerneville, CA 95446 ($1.00) — 3,4,5,6,7,11,19,22, H, P — unique catalog offers old-time varieties of herbs & salad greens with lessons on their history, lore & use — great reading.

HERB GATHERING INC., 5742 Kenwood Ave., Kansas City, MO 64110 ($2.00) — 2,3,4,5,7,10,11,113,19,22 — gourmet vegetables & herb seeds.

J. L. HUDSON SEEDSMAN, P.O. Box 1058, Redwood City, CA 94064 ($1.00) — 3,4,9,10,11,12,13,18,19,21,22 H, P — 103p catalog "a world seed service," offers rare vegetables, herbs, flowers & decorative plants from around the world.

D. LANDRETH SEED CO., P.O. Box 6426, Baltimore, MD 21230 ($2.00) — 1,2,3,4,5,6,7,10,11,12,13,14,19,21, 22 H — you can purchase your seeds from the same company that George Washington & Thomas Jefferson used. Now in its 203rd year, Landreth offers a variety of old-time vegetables.

LE JARDIN DU GOURMET, Box 213, West Danville, VT 05873 (50¢) — 1,2,3,4,5,6,7,8,10,12,17,19,21,22 — a great variety of European and unusual vegetable & herb seeds in *inexpensive (22¢) packets.*

LE MARCHE SEEDS INTERNATIONAL, P.O. Box 190, Dixon, CA 95620 (2.00) — 1,2,3,4,6,7,12,13,14,15,19,22 H, P — beautiful 48p catalog offers seeds, planting advice, lore and recipes for a wide range of French heirloom and hard-to-find vegetables and herbs.

LIBERTY SEED CO., Box 806, New Philadelphia, OH 44663 — 2,4,5,7,10,11,12,13,14,22 — traditional vegetable & flower seeds and accessories.

PARK SEED COMPANY INC., P.O. Box 31, Greenwood, SC 29648-0031 — 2,4,5,7,8,9,11,12,19,22 P — 124p, full color, full line catalog of vegetables, flowers, herbs, fruits, tools, accessories & books.

PINE TREE GARDEN SEEDS, RR No. 1, Box 397, New Gloucester, ME 04260 — 1,2,3,4,6,7,10,11,12,13,14,19,21 H, P — 120p catalog offers 512 varieties of vegetables, herbs, flowers, bulbs, decorative plants, garden tools, great gadgets & one of the best selections of garden books you'll ever find.

PORTER & SON, SEEDMAN, Box 104, Stephenville, TX 76401 — 10,12 — 48p, full line catalog with vegetables, flowers, tools, accessories & books for Texas and southern gardeners.

SOUTHERN EXPOSURE SEED EXCHANGE, P.O. Box 158, North Garden, VA 22959 ($2.00) — 7,10,11,12,19 H, P — 64p catalog offers a great variety of rare vegetables, many developed specifically for the mid-Atlantic region. Their "family heirloom" varieties are just that — vegetables that have been nurtured by individual families for generations for their special qualities. This catalog is a valuable source of information on planting & growing vegetables & on saving seeds.

FRED STOKER & SONS, R. 1, P.O. Box 707, Dresden TN 38225-0707 — H — tobacco plus 16 varieties of sweet potatoes & yams including some "old-time" varieties.

STOKES SEEDS INC., Box 548, Buffalo, NY 14240 — •

2,3,4,5,6,7,12,13,14,23 — full line 164p catalog with 1600 varieties of vegetables & flowers.

TERRITORIAL SEEDS CO., Box 17, Corane, OR 97451 — 2,4,7,19 H — specializes in vegetables for cold, wet climates. Catalog offers seeds, tools, books & accessories.

THOMPSON & MORGAN INC., P.O. Box 1308, Jackson, NJ 08527 — 1,2,3,4,5,7,8,10,11,12,13,14,15,16,19,20,21, 22 — the world's largest seed catalog, at 226p, offers 4000 varieties of flowers & vegetables.

WILLWHITE SEED CO., P.O. Box 23, Poolville, TX 76-76 — P — 52p, full color catalog offers 350 varieties.

◆ ◆ ◆ ◆ ◆

GOOD READING

• • • • •

THE BACKYARD HOMESTEAD, MINI FARM & GAR-
DEN LOG BOOK, by John Jeavons, J. Morgodor Griffin &
Robin Leler, a record book, calendar and guide to an
efficient homestead, 224p, softcover, $8.95 + 1.00 p&h —
Ten Speed Press, Box 7123, Berkeley, CA 94707

A BOOK OF COUNTRY THINGS, Told by Walter
Needham and recorded by Barrows Mussey. Vivid recollec-
tions of 19th Century farm life, 158p, softcover, $6.95 +
1.50 p&h — The Stephen Green Press, Viking Penguin Inc.,
299 Murray Hill Pky., East Rutherford, NJ 07073

THE COMPLETE BOOK OF EDIBLE LANDSCAPING,
by Rosalind Creasy, a guide to using vegetables, fruits, nuts
and herbs in the home landscape, valuable to all vegetable
gardeners for its extensive lists of resources and information on planting and using unusual vegetables, 379p,
softcover, $14.95 + 3.00 p&h — Sierra Club Books, 1142
West Indian School Road, Phoenix, AZ 85103

THE COUNTRY GARDENERS ALMANAC, by Martin
Lawrence, a complete calendar of gardening chores with
practical advice culled from 19th Century farm journals,
224p, softcover, $9.95 + 1.75 p&h — The Main Street
Press, William Case House, Pittstown, NJ 08867

COUNTRY PATTERNS, A Sampler of 19th Century
American Home and Landscape Design, edited by Donald
J. Berg, 128p, softcover, $8.95 + 1.75 p&h — The Main
Street Press, William Case House, Pittstown, NJ 08867

COUNTRY WISDOM, an Almanac of Weather Signs, Moon
Lore, Rural Remedies, Fishing and Hunting Facts, Country
Recipes, Rules of Thumb & Advice on Mother Nature's
Methods, by Jerry Mack Johnson, 154p, hardcover, $6.95
+ 1.50 p&h — Jerry Mack Johnson, Box 5200, San Angelo,
TX 76902

COUNTRY WISDOM BULLETINS, 97 different, 32p booklets with practical how-to advice on home energy, food gardening, maintenance, cooking, preserving and old-time crafts — Storey Communications, School House Road, Pownal, VT 05261

THE DIRECTORY OF SEED & NURSERY CATALOGS, lists close to 400 sources of vegetable seeds, fruit trees, herbs, wildflowers and garden tools, $4.00 postpaid — National Gardening Association, 180 Flynn Ave., Burlington, VT 05401

THE FORGOTTEN ARTS: GROWING, GARDENING AND COOKING WITH HERBS, by Richard M. Bacon, a practical manual with recipes, 128p, softcover, $6.95 + 1.00 p&h — Yankee Books, Box F, Depot Square, Peterborough, NH 03458

GARDENING BY MAIL, by Barbara J. Barton, a directory of over 300 garden suppliers, horticultural societies and libraries throughout the U.S. and Canada, $18.00, postpaid — Tusker Press, P.O. Box 597004, San Francisco, CA 94159

THE GARDEN SEED INVENTORY, edited by Kent Whealy, a list of non-hybrid vegetable seeds available from over 200 seed catalogs, $12.50 — Seed Savers Exchange, 203 Rural Ave., Decorah, IA 52101

GROWING AND SAVING VEGETABLE SEEDS, by Marc Rogers, 144p, softcover, $7.95 + 2.00 p&h — Garden Way Publishing/Storey Communications, School House Road, Pownal, VT 05261

THE HEIRLOOM GARDENER, by Carolyn Jabs, how to grow and save heirloom vegetables with descriptions & illustrations from 19th Century seed catalogs and garden books, 310p, softcover, $9.95 + 3.00 p&h — Sierra Club Books, 1142 West Indian School Road, Phoenix, AZ 85103

THE HEIRLOOM VEGETABLE GARDEN, by Roger A. Kline, Robert F. Becker and Lynne Belluscio, information on growing and preparing 36 popular 19th Century vegetables, from period garden books, 28p, softcover, $3.00 — Department of Vegetable Crops, Cornel University, Ithaca, NY 14853

HOMESTEAD HINTS*, A Compendium of Useful Information from the Past for the Home, Garden and Household, edited by Donald J. Berg, 128p, softcover, $6.95 + 1.00 p&h — Ten Speed Press, Box 7123, Berkeley, CA 94707

HOW TO BUILD IN THE COUNTRY*, Good Advice from the Past on How to Choose a Site, Plan, Design, Build, Landscape & Furnish Your Home in the Country, edited by Donald J. Berg, 128p, softcover, $6.95 + 1.00 p&h — Ten Speed Press, Box 7123, Berkeley, CA 94707

HOW TO GROW MORE VEGETABLES than You Ever Thought Possible on Less Land Than You Can Imagine, by John Jeavons, a concise guide to the Biodynamic/French Intensive Method of Vegetable Gardening, 159p, softcover, $8.95 + 1.00 p&h — Ten Speed Press, Box 7123, Berkeley, CA 94707

SAVING SEEDS, A Farm and Home Gardener's Guide, by Stephen R. Cain, a 20p guide to saving seeds with an emphasis on Heirloom varieties, $10.00 (includes 1yr subscription to the newsletter "The Heirloom Gardener") — Center for the Study of the American Family Farm, Rt. 2, Box 44, New Market, VA 22844

THE SEED FINDER, by John Jeavons and Robin Leler, a source-book of "Heirloom" seeds and plants that are available today. Developed before uniformity and durability for shipping were of prime importance, old-time vegetables are often better tasting than their modern counterparts. Selections of traditional shade trees, decorative shrubs and flowers give authenticity to a historic

home's landscape. 160p, softcover, $4.95 + 1.00 p&h —
Ten Speed Press, Box 7123, Berkeley, CA 94707

THE VEGETABLE GARDEN, by MM Vilmorin-Andrieux,
a direct reprint of the authoritative, 1885 book with
complete directions on the culture and use of hundreds of
old-time varieties of vegetables & herbs, 620p, softcover,
over 650 illustrations, $11.95 + 1.00 p&h — Ten Speed
Press, Box 7123, Berkeley, CA 94707

◆ ◆ ◆

*THE KITCHEN GARDENER'S GUIDE is the latest book
in Donald Berg's "Homestead Hints" series published by
Ten Speed Press. The first two titles are HOW TO BUILD
IN THE COUNTRY and HOMESTEAD HINTS.

INDEX

• • • • •

Donald J. Berg, an architect, has edited eleven books on yesterday's homes and gardens. His column, "Homestead Hints," appears in newspapers across the country. Every year he, his wife, Christine, and their three children plant and tend a vegetable garden. From time to time they even get some vegetables.

• • • • •